THE COMPLETE POEMS OF NATHANIEL HUTNER

Books by Nathaniel Hutner

Heracleitus Under Water   1988

War: A Book Of Poems   2003

The Name We Never Lose   2019

❧

Plays by Nathaniel Hutner

Godot Arrives

Godot Imagine Godot

Godot at Night

Godot, Alive or Dead

The President Pardons Godot

Monks on Love

❧

Short Plays by Nathaniel Hutner

Hot Potatoes

The Fix

Keewaydin Plays

THE COMPLETE POEMS OF NATHANIEL HUTNER

Onion River Press

Burlington, Vermont

Some of the poems which appear in this volume first appeared in the following periodicals: *The Yale Review*: Revenge; *POETALK - Bay Area Poets' Coalition*: A Zen State, Lucretia Locuples, Leider, True Tooth; *Chrysanthemum*: Other; *Breakthrough*: Heracleitus Under Water.

Copyright © 2021 by Nathaniel Hutner

All rights reserved. No part of this publication may be reproduced, distributed, or transmitted in any form or by any means, including photocopying, recording, or other electronic or mechanical methods, without the prior written permission of the publisher, except in the case of brief quotations embodied in critical reviews and certain other noncommercial uses permitted by copyright law.

Onion River Press
191 Bank Street
Burlington, VT 05401

Names: Hutner, Nathaniel, author.
Title: The complete poems of Nathaniel Hutner / Nathaniel Hutner.
Description: Includes index. | Burlington, VT: Onion River Press, 2021.
Identifiers: LCCN: 2020921277 | ISBN: 978-1-949066-58-6
Subjects: LCSH American poetry. | Poetry--21st century. | BISAC POETRY / American / General.
Classification: LCC PS3608.U862 C66 2021 | DDC 811.6--dc23

Designed by Jenny Lyons, Middlebury VT

Printed in the United States of America

First Edition 2021

To the memory of my mother and father

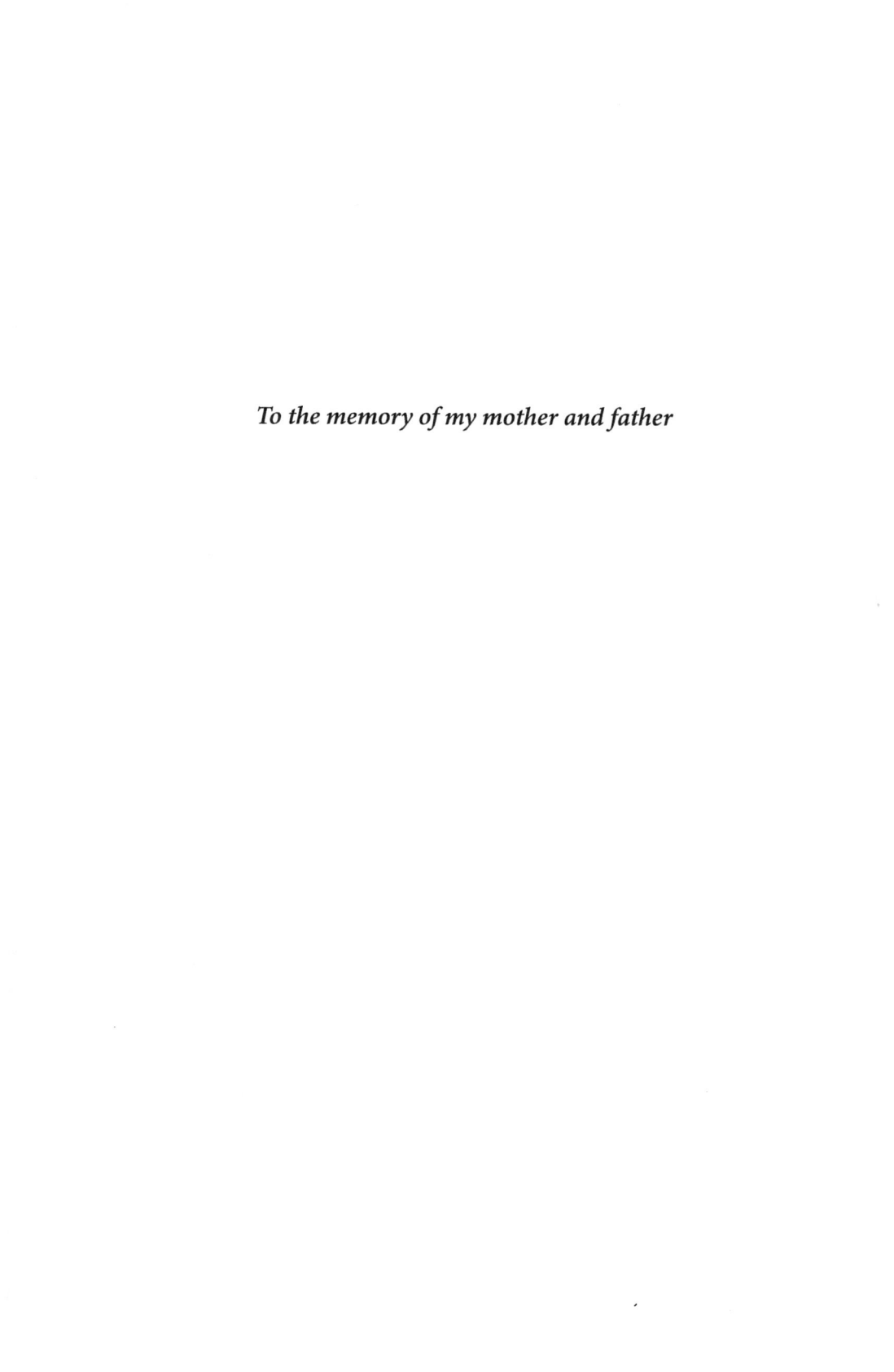

CONTENTS

HERACLEITUS UNDER WATER

Zanzibar	3
The Sea-Dragon	4
I would like to feel completely well	5
True Tooth	6
I tie my ear to a balloon	7
Sculpt Me	8
The Musical Air	9
A Long Key	10
Here in the Market	11
Time to Beguine	12
A Green Bird and an Answer	13
In the spring	14
Blue Leaf	15
Gossip Mongers	16
Words in Winter I	17
Words in Winter II	18
Self-Portrait	19
Heracleitus Under Water	20
The New Renaissance Man	21
Fee Simple	23
Orpheus	24
Dido	25
The night becomes my soul	26
Antigone	27
Le Roi des Fauves	28

TRIPS

Dalliance by the Daisies	37
Your Answer?	38
Preface to a Play	39
A Pluralistic Universe	40
Christmas	41
General Breed	42
Trees	43
Cracking Up	44
A Gain on Rain	45
Vision	46
Slide by Me	47
Trouble Spots in the Field of Vision	48
A Philosophical Greek	49
Pope	50
A Greek God	51
Now Reason's Drowned…	52
Against the Academic	53
Thrice Three Makes Nine…	54
Name-Dropping	55
A Danube?	56
Lupine	57
Family Collage	58
A Drama of the Plathian Interior	59
This Sky Is My Turn…	60
A Lie About You	61
A Blue Belly for Odysseus	62
If It Did, I Was Cold	63
Rose Blind	64
Duplicate	65
Politics or the Great Bird	66
Buckets of Love	67

Our Rose Poem	68
A Small Box	69
The Shy One	70
Lovage	71
Cold Stone	72
What We Wish	73
Ha-Ha's	74
Pure as Pain	75
Pale Apothecaries	76
Two by Four	77
God Can Take Care of Himself	78
"Tityre, Tu Patulae Recubans Sub Tegmine Fagi..."	79
Shadows of the Evening	80
A Certain Heaviness on the Tongue	82
Phasellus Ille Quem Videtis Hospites Ait Fuisse Navium Celerrimus	83

LOVE 2

Love 2	89
Aces	91
Address to a Failed Apocalypse	93
A Short Present	94
It Doesn't Pay to Go to Princeton Anymore	95
Ocean Agonistes	96
Sappho	97
Maidenhair	98
Possible Tête-a-Tête	99
A Dream	100
There We Go	102
The Kiss	104
Nightcap	106
Terminal	108
To His Love	109

Blue Rotation	111
Collegium Vitae	113
Mother's Day, 2000	114
Woe	116
I Need the Rest	118
The Ear-Ring	120
The Heart's Graces	122
Saved Beneath the Season	124
A Cold Complaint	126
The Rue Poem	128
Wednesday's Treasures	130
A Pragmatic Ideal	132
Ode	133
Time Is Falling Down	135
The Present	136
Regina is the Fault	138
Blasting	140
Babies	141
Doubles	143
Bounce	145
What Do You Remember?	147
Prolegomena to Any Future Metaphysic	149
How We End Up	151
Time In	153
Waiting/Repulsed	155
Hiding Light	157
A Vision	159
Southampton	161
Periandros	162
Pretty Pike	164
Goodbye, Dog	166
The Pilot	167

Empty Hazard	168
Night Light	169
Dalliance	171
Tragedy Turns Away	173

WAR

The Story of My Life	179
Whose Horseman?	181
War	183
Going Up	185
I Have Saved a Life	187
The Charming Face of Dawn	189
Laurels	191
Complaint	193
The Trap	195
Amplification	197
I Am Going	199
Lip-Sync	201
The Blue Parrot	203
Looking Up an Old Friend	205
The Title of Discernment	207
I Loll on Lily-Pads	209
Recovering	211
To His Muse	213
Spring in May	215
In Line	217
Traveling Light	219
No Title for Me	221
The Able Man	223
Light Me Up	225
Malaise	227
Coney Island	229
A Song Aside	231

THE SHADOW BOOK

Johannesburg	237
Specific Gravity	247
Another End	249
I Cry Inside	250
The Old Tooth	251
Psychopharmaceutical	252
Are There Strawberries in Heaven?	253
United Untied	255
A Drink	257
The Masked Move	258
Liquefaction of the Mass	260
The Ballistic Partisan	262
Say Nothing	263
The Shadow Poem	264
Passing	265
The Mourning Doves	267
A Plaint	268
The Loss	269
Our Backyard	271
The Pink Period I	272
The Pink Period II	274
The Rainbow	276
A Long Walk	278
Who There Is	280
The Pyre	283
The Lily on My Hat	284
My Practical Pentagon	285
Empty Beside	286
Troubles Leaving	288
The Wan Ride	289
Polarization	291

In the Chambers of the Dark ... 293
Lipitor ... 294
I Am Thinking ... 295
High Tea ... 296
Paradise ... 297
Hanging on the Ruins of My Nose ... 298
Hot ... 299
Kissing a Kiss ... 300
Left in the Order of Things ... 301
Looking Back ... 302
Follow Me ... 303
Signature ... 304
Honey-Suckle ... 305
Fin de Parti ... 306
I Must Understand ... 307
Will You Sink With Me? ... 308
Disavowing the Mean ... 309
Maybe I Can Squeeze ... 310

RAIN AS ART

Rain as Art ... 315
Operator ... 316
If I Start in on You ... 318
A Little Clip ... 320
A Man Without a Tongue ... 321
Papa ... 322
Well ... 323
Patient Days ... 324
Nonnulla ... 325
The Phoenix and the Dove ... 326
Mandarin ... 327
Poetry ... 328
Prunella ... 329

Ode to Time 330
On the Road 331
Sex Pain 333
Chrysanthemum 334
The Vortices 335
A Declining Star 336
No Time Left 337
The Wounds of Time 338
Debts 339
Row 340
Proceed, Wish 341
At the Age of Five 342
Pepsico Pipelines, Coca-Cola Conduits 343
What Will Happen? 344
Bruegellande 345
Chanticleer 346
A Shady Terminus 347
Forty 348
Where Did He Go? 349
Period of Treasure 350
The Question 351
They 352
Time Again 353
Enemy 354
Try Tea 355
L'avenir 356
Epithalamium 357

YOUTH AND AGE

Youth and Age 361
The Ultimatum 363
Listening 364
Rounding Out 365

A Sallow Season	366
The Bee Dying	367
Etwas, Zum Beispiel	368
Love Is Like…	370
Free for Fame or Fame for Free	371
Some Day I Will Stop	373
Faces	375
Big Birth	377
Peonies	378
Apostrophe	380
The Voice of Silence	381
Look, Mother	383
Hours of an Age	385
The Dead Dog	387
I Rightly Fly	389
Painting Late	391
The Critic	393
Sparrow Fleeing	395
Work	397
Exit at Birth	398
The Drowned Turk	400
A Meditation	402
Conspire With My Heart	404
Global Warming	406
The Choir of the Mind	408
Pleasant, the Wind	410
A Blue Time	412
The Tides	414
Halloween	416
Rembrandt or Vermeer	418
A Sip at the End	420
A Rough Pass	422

THE LUNGWORT AND THE HELLEBORE

The Lungwort and the Hellebore	427
Mister Apollo	428
Summer Sunflowers	429
Visiting Time	430
Where Am I?	431
Socrates' Apology	432
The Peach Tree Grows	434
The Dove and I	435
Advent	437
What They Didn't Want	438
Painting a Lady	440
Off We Go	441
A Mystery Slow To Be Realized	443
Blessing	445
We Walk Down the Strand	447
The Injured Eye	449
They Don't Know	451
Philosophy	453
A Grave Situation	455
Snow	457
Floating on the Water	459
Intemperate Weather	461
In Hawaii	463
A Single Summer	465
The Book	467
Visions Out of Africa	469
The Gift	471
Iraq Compos Mentis	472
What the Fool Could Tell	480
Then the Full Love	481
Grass	482
Harvest	483

THE NAME WE NEVER LOSE

Kill Me Now 487
What My Love Will Send to Me 488
Underground 489
Kiss, Kiss 490
December 491
The Archbishop in Spite of Himself 492
And for Dessert… 493
The Name We Never Lose 494
Hippocrates 497
Dibble-Dabble 498
Summertime 499
Trouble 500
Pearls 501
Trying to Hide? 502
Twins 503
Apple Trip 504
Other 506
Primus Inter Pares 507
A Plangent Tear 508
Naked for a Day 509
Vertical Alert 510
Ode to Water 511
Self Delivery 513
Alabama in Painting 514
Opuscular Thoughts 516
Feline Maintenance 517
Color Role 518
A Short Translation 519
Doubt 520
Working Out Parallels 521
Naked 522

Obligato	523
Prolixin	524
A Hard Rap	525
My Nocturnal Migrations	526
The Mirror and the Mask	527
A Million Spots	528
Buying Nothing	529
A Zen State	530
Lucretia Locuples	531
Leider	532
Revenge	533
Love	534

ALL IS WELL

All Is Well	539
Jesus!	540
We Sing	541
The Safe Song	542
Sighing Lightly in the Dark	543
They Called Her Flower	544
If Only for a Drink	545
Ditty	546
Arrival/Departure	547
Tears Hot, Tears Cold	548
Lip Shift	549
Hiding in the Light	550
Black at Dawn	551
Take Help From Both Sides	552
Prelude and Performance	553
Love by Increments	554
Curbside	555
Living Extensively	556
Infinity	557

Rich Text	558
The Skin of Eel	559
Honey-Suckle	560
You Run Slowly Down	561
Resurrection	562
Disavowing the Last	563
Freeing the Oysters	564
Off We Go	565
Night Song	566
Tour of the Fortunate	567
To a Wild Rose	568
Where He Go, That Man?	570
Illustrious Plum	571
Yellow Umbrella	572
Sleep's Canon	573
Led by the Nose	574
Allo!	575
Good-Bye!	576
A Big Matisse	577
Plunkett	578
Cool Fracture	579
"Get Demobbed!" She Said	580
One Whole Chronicler of the Race	581
Ectoplasmic	582
Home	583
Song 1	584
Breath of Fear	585
A Cure	586
The Bandit and the Pericole	588
Panjandrum	589
Bleu	590
Where O Wisdom?	591
Life Lost	592

Prodigal	593
A John	594
Elephant	595
Terrible Truths	597
Amber Motes	598
Plotinus' Emanations	599
Character Store	600
Dance, Dear	601
Nothing, My Love	602
Pinstripe	603
Hello, Man	604
Dead	605
Turtle Dove	607
Sweet Prince, I Cannot See	608
Hello	610
Birthday	611
Run Like a Hawk	612
Prinz of the Realm	613
Dali	614
Readymade	615
Apologia	616
The End of Time	617
Pinckney Born Again	618
Waste	619
Revelation	620
Holy Love	621
Painting the Lady in a Blue Trellis	622
Love Has Its Colors, Too	623
Losing	624
Jewel of a Carriage	625
To Alice	626
The Lover Escapes	627
Premature	628

The Head	629
The Artist: Femme Assise	630
Forgive the Right and Left	631
A Swift Purchase	633
Hello, Miro	634
Picasso Bends	635
Hiring Man	636
Hanging Man	637
Arise, Chagall	638
Barley Corn	639
Halfway There	640
Trashed	641
Sixdenier	642
The Blithedale Romance	645
Index of First Lines	*647*
Index of Titles	*661*

Preface

As the generation of Eliot's successors dies off, modern poetry seems in danger of losing its voice. American poets have taken to murmuring to themselves in safe and unobtrusive meters; they have become relaxed and conversational; it doesn't matter whether they are raking leaves in a suburb or rubbing sticks in a cell on Mount Athos, everything inspires the same mild remarking, the same soft meandering lines. This sort of poetry can be pleasant enough when it is well done – at its best it has the effect of rain on a tent roof – but it turns to vapor once we put down the book and go about our business. We turn to the first poem in this first collection, however, and read –

> Soon we will go to Zanzibar
> And live upon cinnamon.
> Or we will float like the lotus
> Down the Nile, wise as rain,
> Or pursue gazelles across the Africque plain,
> Or we will seize the temple at Thebes
> And astonish the Greeks …

And find that we are listening to a voice that does not let us go so easily. It is a voice that belongs to a poet who has put himself to school with some difficult masters – Beckett, Eliot and Stevens immediately suggest themselves – and come out confidently singing his own song. It is alternately grave and playful, fluid yet always tightly controlled. It is a voice that has authority. Some of the poems in this collection are difficult and "modern", holding back their full meaning from the casual reader; others are as easy and unassuming as a nursery rhyme; but they all have that indefinable timbre that marks them as coming from an accomplished craftsman working his gift with great intensity of spirit.

The last thing I want to do is to "explicate" any of the poems in this collection. I would rather try to suggest some of the larger tendencies in Hutner's verse without doing critical violence to any individual poem. The first thing that strikes me about his poems is the quality of the imagination which produced them. It is a transfiguring imagination. We see it at work most clearly in the poems about nature. Some poets, like William Carlos Williams, take a walk and see a tree, and the tree remains a tree when he writes about it. But Hutner is among those poets who are interested in the essence of things; a piece of nature for him breaks down into form and color, light and shade; he sees it in a way that is highly personal, not to say idiosyncratic, but also in a way which somehow answers to our own most furtive impressions:

> *White fire of dew*
> *On leaves, white steel*
> *Of dew, turn to ice*
> *On fallen trees,*
> *Turn to ice in fall.*

What is true of nature is true of the "self" in these poems. Hutner is writing at what is probably the end of the age of confessional poetry, inaugurated by Snodgrass and Lowell in the fifties, and some of his work partakes in this tradition. But his poems are a far cry from the mannered revelations of Lowell's imitators ("Mother, that day you and father/took me to the lake…"). No, the "self" in Hutner's poems, stuck though it is among life's messy contingencies, is a higher and more universal affair than we are accustomed to finding in contemporary anthologies; its plight is to some extent the plight of any intelligent and sensitive soul grappling with the modern world. There is despair, but there is also affirmation, and the two are inseparable, like reverse sides of a coin. The poet understands with the late Yeats that true affirmation is closely related to a tragic sense of life; he feels this in his gut and not as an intellectual abstraction. Behind the rich coloration of Hutner's poems – and the virtuosic manipulation of color is one of his most distinctive stylistic traits – there is blackness, but this blackness is like the blacking in a mirror which allows it to reflect the colors of a spring day.

Unlike the persona in most post-war poetry, whose creators have difficulty getting outside their own skulls, the self in these poems is not a world unto itself. It is open and grasping; it has feelers extending everywhere, reaching out to nature and back through history. It is remarkable, in fact, the way history ("Ancestors and broils intestine/The whole old story of the race") keeps intruding into these poems. This is not common in American letters and requires a deeply attuned imagination, because this richly endowed, somewhat shallow country in which we live has thus far been spared the meatgrinder of what most peoples at most times have experienced as History.

The self in these poems is doing exactly what Rilke advised to a young German poet; his is not grasping for the easy answers, but rather living the questions themselves until they turn of their own accord into answers. The answers will no doubt be different from what was expected, and the poet is not a little impatient for their arrival. In the meantime, some of the questions are barely supportable, with the result that many of the lines in these poems hit the reader like shrapnel from what the poet calls the 'exploded self':

> *Who will love me when I, too, am black at heart?*
>
> *Now the venom of our present is at work.*

But there is always nature to interpose a little ease, and we don't have to go far to find other lines in which a lighter mood predominates:

> *the amber-backed bull-frog blows his note*
> *against the sky*
> *and proudly declares himself paterfamilias*
> *over the primary grades of Lamarck's*
> *hierarchy of beasts;*
> *the spider tries out his toes*
> *in a little aerial ballet*
> *as he spins his first web*
> *of the season, in which,*
> *if he's lucky, he'll catch*
> *bluebottles and bees…*

It is difficult to know where to stop quoting some of the poems in this volume. Many of the lines stick like burrs and are difficult to shake off. It is worth noting, however, that the best poems in this collection are the most recent. There is much to look forward to from this gifted poet.

George Sim Johnston

THE COMPLETE POEMS OF NATHANIEL HUTNER

To the Reader,

The poems contained herein date to the troubles at Harvard University in the spring of 1969. In May of that year, the police invaded Harvard yard and carted off a large number of protesters. The following morning I found myself standing in front of Widener Library alone, shocked by what I had seen happen. I returned to my rooms in Greenough Hall and composed my first poem:

LET DAY ARISE

Let day arise
And try to chase the shadow of our soul
To its demise
Upon the rocks of reason risen whole

From night, invoked
By minds that cling to it fanatically,
Now having choked
Upon the senses' food to cling perpetually.

Let day arise
So partisans of either side may play with words,
Truth dies,
And pathos turns to bathos in dismay.

This poem was the first of my career and convinced me that I should never abandon poetry. From the age of eighteen until the age of sixty-eight, I wrote. The other poem that comes to mind when I contemplate this volume is the following:

> The night becomes my soul,
> The day my empty whole,
> In myself my ghost,
> To others the most
> Of what I am and am not.

After a long life I have come to accept what I am. I hope that the poems give pleasure and instruction.

Nathaniel Hutner

Heracleitus Under Water
: 1988 :

ZANZIBAR

Soon we will go to Zanzibar
And live upon cinnamon,
Or we will float like the lotus
Down the Nile, wise as rain,
Or pursue gazelles across the Afrique plain,
Or we will seize the temple at Thebes
And astonish the Greeks
With the length of our feet.
How wide is your head? we'll ask,
And laugh.
My head would a suit a bonnet for two,
Or two-and-a-half.
There is really no way to say
What we'll do,
Though I know incontrovertibly
I cannot do it without you.

THE SEA-DRAGON

I am waiting, patient.
I am going to fish.
I am going to find
A sea-dragon on my line.
He will have eyes like knives,
A mouth greater than grief,
And each of his many scales
Bright as a viper's teeth.

It would please me if, without being dined upon,
I could love this fish as it would wish.

I would like to feel completely well,
Like a young tamarisk tree,
Or a carillon of banging Russian bells.
Who will see my inside when I am out
Posturing in the dark?
Who will love me when I, too, am black at heart?
These are questions I have never dared to ask.
To whom can I vouchsafe my past?
There is not much in it for anyone:
A blind eye and exploded self.
I'll try to help
Myself as well as others. I promise not to hide
Behind reticences and the innocence of a child.
We all have much, I am sure, to bear,
As for me, I can say, 'I'm still here'.

TRUE TOOTH

Suppose, to start with,
A curve, of any nature,
Apple or plum,
Or what you think will do,
And then cut infinitely deep
Like a tooth:

Pit desire against itself
With care, light the fire,
And listen. What can we hear
In the flame? Its blue stands
For truth, not the blues,
And as we burn with the flame,
The blue becomes ever deeper
And transparent as Heaven.

I tie my ear to a balloon.
From above it hears
The music of a broom.
Someone is sweeping below the moon,
I think it is the mistress
Of a poet's doom.

SCULPT ME

Sculpt me, turn me on the wheel,
As the world spins, I begin to heal,
There is an art to how I feel,
Sculpt me, turn me, make me real.

THE MUSICAL AIR

The musical air turns wisdom to wit,
Draws laughter down to earth
And sanctifies it,
Humour is purified by way of pain,
Sun makes the poppy grow —
And so does the rain.

A LONG KEY

A poem exhibits different colors
At different angles. Each thought

Provokes its cousins variously, setting up
Dependencies like prophecies or memories.

HERE IN THE MARKET

Here in the market
There is flesh for you:
Amber, gold, saffron,
All shades of the sun
Save the sun that sets
In red and royal purple.
We'll take a hand in the
Planting and learn to dive
Deep into the soul
And return with the
One gift worth giving:
And that is life.

TIME TO BEGUINE

Said Sweeney to Mrs. Porter,
I shall swill your soda-water,
And then lie dead-drunk
in your lap,
My eye-lids open to your
charms.

Mrs. Porter was having none of it.
"Tut," she said,
"You are, as far as the eye can see,
King of the Egyptians,
And I am your faithful adhaerens,
Stuck to you
like glue
(What a mess!)"

"We shall have to do a bit piece,
A clean-up campaign,
With the field open
To all comers
And other prepotent people."

And so they did.

A GREEN BIRD AND AN ANSWER

Where there is love
There you have a green bird
And an answer.
The green bird
Is a parrot
who sighs at night,
and tells you what you say.
It never flies,
and lives on a chain.
The answer gives you silence,
and sleeps into the twilight of the new day.
It is without dread.
You will see it some time
in the mouth of the loved one,
glistening, a tooth at a time,
in the dark.
It will tell you
where to find yourself,
and give you a bed in old age.
It is never tired,
and leaves youth
only to see
what can be made
of a green bird in the shade.

In the spring
lily-of-the-valley
blows white against the green
leaves of the eiderdown pansies;
squirrels deliberate over their infidelities,
and teach their children how to tease
nuts out of trees;
the amber-backed bull-frog blows his note
against the sky
and proudly declares himself paterfamilias
over the primary grades of Lamarck's
hierarchy of beasts;
the spider tries out his toes
in a little aerial ballet
as he spins his first web
of the season, in which,
if he's lucky, he'll catch
bluebottles and bees;
in the spring, the age
is awake again,
and sings itself to sleep every evening
with a song from Corinthians
on love.

BLUE LEAF

Blue leaf leave me,
Blue metal on the lawn,
The long way down
Is new to me
Though not new at all.

White fire of dew
On leaves, white steel
Of dew, turn to ice
On fallen trees,
Turn to ice in fall.

GOSSIP MONGERS

Badinage behind the back
Is elastic. Yesterday's cruel news
Will feed today's sod

Anytime. The greater the better.
A bulletin from the front
Is no good. What we need

Is laughter and a cynic's grin.
Then we'll do each other in.
There's no other way to win.

So much for love.

WORDS IN WINTER I

Out by the gas-house
the parlour-maid laughs
and says 'speak to me'

Words fall
Autumn closes up shop

A sweet tongue will talk all you want
even in winter, under leaves

poplar leaves no ash in the grate

A rating's a sailor by day
— but by night?

Out by the gas-house
the parlour-maid laughs
and says 'speak to me'

WORDS IN WINTER II

The words won't go in,
The cerebellum's a jelly,
Images flock to the shadows
and hide in black overcoats,
beating out the breath of life
into the cold, smoking
in the dark, wavering
between 'yes' and 'no'.
So much for the golden-toed tongue
that used to dance across the snow
under the white sun;
Now the venom of our present is at work,
the singing's stopped,
the seer's gone home,
the music's in the ear alone;
What sound will save us now?

SELF-PORTRAIT

Born by woodbine
In biennial pomp,
Puck's progeny,
Amber and androgynous,
A two-eyed allegorical Damascene
Alive at night:
  Circe's phantasy
  Christ's eye

HERACLEITUS UNDER WATER

Antiquities live off fat,
As the burnished breast will tell you,
Falling flaccid at the rise of age.
Three pebbles in a stream will tell you,
Burnished by the wave, how to hold out
Until the end, living under water,
Round with age.

So we see the polished chronometer
Of the stream's bed, lying under the lithe body
Of the water, into which we step
Again and again,
But never into the same.

THE NEW RENAISSANCE MAN

The new Renaissance man
Shocks the populace,
Poopoos their irregular cry to their face,
Turns his collar round,
Salutes the night-drake and the lunar owl,
Knocks the old stage down
and sets a new one up.

Who's heard the dirge?
Not a one:
salutary salus mortis,
an ignis fatuus,
and Fate play pins
on the head of a desolate whore.

    At the window sits
A dried prig,
A flower of youth fit
For a late grave,
Skin, bones, and a wig,
And eyes that see everything
And sing of anything they see

        Is there season in the spring,
        Or drought in the summer,
        Or draught in the fall,
        Or death in the winter?

Perfection dries on the vine,
The vain glorify themselves,
The accountable turn to stone.
    So goes esteem.

    I am Shelley
    come again, come again, come again
    I am
    come again
    and lost to the

FEE SIMPLE

Publish perceptible
Perversions accredited
Corybantic crows

Kill time and die
dear Mr. Butterfly
"perhaps he's lapsed"
that's me
    Dance to the new time
    rag.

Catch a hag and bag her,
Peas pour mon pot.
Grass,
Demystified, dried.

POLICE LEAVE PREMISES BEREAVED

The triple prick of platinum
That nature gave me for a tongue:
Time to Metternich, Shakespeare and Pound.

ORPHEUS

Orpheus, lute on a string,
Eyes of a child,
Sits in the stream
Where lilies smile,
And skeets fly
Over green enamelling,
White-pies and blue anemones,

And sings word-music,
Music to the world
Of dead souls,
Of black blood,
And the inimical chill that flows
From the yellow crusty shell
Of an unknown dead man's skull.

DIDO

Dido died upon the pyre,
Aetherised by love of fire
Or fire of love,
And now she floats
Among us all within the air
In microscopic motes:
We breathe her in and out
and out and in
and never know it.

The night becomes my soul,
The day my empty whole,
To myself my ghost
To others the most
Of what I am and am not.

ANTIGONE

Turn Antigone out.
Let her sleep
With the goat
And the sheep
In the folds
Of her soul
Which she holds
Over foul
Mortality.

Is she gone?
Not undone.

LE ROI DES FAUVES

    Pray, then Purge.
    That sticks.
Lord, give us strength
    Bon courage
    Bonne nuit

Ave verum corpus
Corpulent, assonant, a nance for the asking,
    for the pimping
Here in the light
Dead insight will take us all
    dear Allworthy, no snipe
    don't wipe his nose
    What a rose for a daughter
    What a rose.

Levitate please.
Into the novitiate.
New, youthful, innocent, ripe, prime,
A capital candidate for the one great
    Advocacy.
Called to God.
    By whom?
Good God, He knows?

Leave him to his celibate.
Celebrated rupture, rotund, rolling
Dung dyed.

    Stamped on a bilious ant
    on the —
    no pig's pizzles here.

Alleluia
Alleluia
    Hecabe again?
    Lost with the dead at Troy
The matriarchal head of the Trojan dead.
Deceased or dying?
Decadent at the least
    blind

Pretense. Pure pretense.
    Perhaps the old man's got his cue
    Quoi?
    cure.
Curvilinear carapace — involuntary involution of the
        will
Call it what you will
    What seed to shake here!

Time cures all,
According to the doctrinaire philosopher,
Optimistic prince, practical pauper,
And true believer in a whole soul.

    Who's kept his?
Why the dam on the right.
The wife of a plutocratic king.

    Proserpine, deceased as decreed,
    Craves your ear's
    Good leave to season her history
    With a tear
Her own best parts abandoned
One: the religious
Two: philosophic
Three: the poetic
and now economic
How insensible
Have not found the
Via dolorosa
Not so douloureux
Dear me, sighs, simpers
A simple-witted iamb:
    Hecabe, Hecabe,
    lost her sweet soul,
    Now she's the shadow
    of what she was whole

Intersession sits on her head of state.
Neck and nape mimosa-green,
A median pair of eyes, crepitating,
A long tongue, said to end
in scales, nostrils pervious-windy,
Hair rufous, buff and brown,
Very possibly polygamous
(though the truth has yet to be shown),
Butt thick, bill blunt, head flat,
blotched and depressed,

Exhibiting a conspicuous crest,
A resonant, melancholy wail
varied by a clucking note.
She eats clover, another seven deadly seeds,
and sole.
    Conceives by night.

Back to love in the trenches:
    a true so
    A truth so inimitable
Ah! without peer
    sink wi' th' king
    drown to Phlebas
    a Phlegmatic ass
    as:
        deceit behind a mask
        goodness in craft
        the lordliest
        absurdissimum

give him a pill
give him a purge
    the head's gone
    ergo
    malady's indeterminate
    Elgol in Skye
    certified insane
    a gesture
    to premature
    Russian suppression

      transient, inefficient, capricious

let her glout
sanctified, sacrificial
Pursued to the welkin's cheek
Purely aethereal

    Either or
    non non
    et et
    vel vel

A polyglottal grammar for the
    germane

O whole thou art!
insight sublime
inspired mime
a lunatic tinker taught to drink
that well-beloved assonantal rhyme

well well

Trips
: 1990, 2005 :

DALLIANCE BY THE DAISIES

Tracks of ants around the primrose
Are like premonitory tears in the snow,
Dry in time.
The snipe's cousin has come on a visit.
It is late,
The past is awry,
And the poet
Is too secret for words.

YOUR ANSWER?

Have you ended our affair?
In your throat I feel the air,
You can speak,
I can hear,
Tell me where we go from here:

Nowhere is now what I fear —
"Nowhere, nowhere" in my ear,
A lonely word I cannot bear,
Anywhere —

PREFACE TO A PLAY

This play is a rock
That disturbs the white shore,
We shall not hear
The green sea anymore;

I watch my one play
Form the ribs of the sea,
The ribs ride the water
Asleep on my lee,

Can anyone hear
The doubt in my voice,
Should I choose not to speak
And betray my own choice?

Pain is the pleasure
Of poets, I know,
But times change
With pain and
With poets who grow.

A PLURALISTIC UNIVERSE

The street senses the pedestrian,
The image of holy warfare
On foot; it loves the touch
Of the rubber, the pedestrian
As perpetual lover, leveraged
By weather and a warm coat.
One foot will do it, one foot.

We pass by elaborate passages,
And remain mute.

CHRISTMAS

A teaser, a dwindling dish,
As age develops,
So does my wish:
That all be happy here,
I think can be,
But we must all believe in this
As one, that's you and you and you,
And me.

GENERAL BREED

That is General Breed:
A boiling fixture.
He can develop his eyes
Into wide windows.
I have seen his pupils
Explode.
When they return to earth,
He collects them,
And uses them
To plant trees.

How many General Breeds
Do we need—
And how many
Breedable seeds?

TREES

Wherever soil or stone can nourish,
There grows the silver-tipped hemlock,
The emerald elm, the frangible ash,
Sweet maple and rolling oak,
And the balm
Of the retiring witch-hazel,
The light pine
And stony ironwood,
Aspen and elder,
And tamarack too:
All make a home
For our poet
And for you.

CRACKING UP

Blood as full:
Crack-heads pass it on.
It is beyond them.
It is the Grand Canyon
Of leaks.
They can't retreat.
Is that how they introduce themselves?
Friendly?

A GAIN ON RAIN

Precipitation tickles.
It is heaven touching the head.
In bed we do it finger-tip by finger-tip
And naturalize the color red.
There is room here for moral employment:
How else can we find out enjoyment?
Heaven precipitates freely without fee.
What about you? What about me?

VISION

Theory. An eye into the dark.
We pull the eye apart.
So we may see
Theory in the dark.
That is a black eye.
Blue was invented
For convalescence.
Azure is in.
In what?
People have a problem
With their azure sky.
People have a problem
With their azure eye.

SLIDE BY ME

I have a lion's eyes,
They eat people alive,
Or roast them turn by turn,
It depends how they want to burn,
The wicked tend to fat,
Each one burns like a rat,
And explodes like a Roman candle:

I do this for life,
Not from pride,
What I give you is inside,
I do this because I can't hide,
I see you,
But I cannot see my own eyes.
You are my mirror,
And I know you can't lie.

TROUBLE SPOTS IN THE FIELD OF VISION

There is someone staring at me
From behind: I cannot tell
What he sees, or if he is blind.
If blind, he may feel like me,
And then excuse himself and lie
About what he has just surmised of us
In his mind's eye.

I am new to this game of Truth,
I am the blind man, but I shall try
To see what goes on inside of me
When I feel like you and lie.

A PHILOSOPHICAL GREEK

logically marine
marooned between
thought and thing:
a perspicuous recipe designed
to make the sight blind
the blind see
and the seen unseen.
    Let us have three.
A theoretical canticle
From abstract to superficies:

> Out of amber out of snout,
> nursing gander, gore and gout,
> pursestrings of a wicked Jew,
> jewels of an antique dame,
> daughter of Jerusalem,
> In the mind deposit all,
> Illuminate, extinguish and absolve.

POPE

Give him a death's head,
The dead head deposed,
Reposed, reflected, sighed,
Sighs, picks his nose,
Prepares for the play,
Yawns imperturbably.

Twist my ear
Twine my hair
Turn my eye
No light here
Preserve a poor man's equanimity.

A GREEK GOD

The cross-piece of his bow
bends in the sun,
The moon sits on his left side at night,
His children are the signs of the zodiac,
each one engraved on his brow;
His hair billows behind him,
a fine grey wave
flowing in a circle
round the world

We gave him time
and he died

Now all that's left is
the dust of the universe
settling slowly on our heads,
If you breathe carefully
you can fill your lungs
with what's left of a dead race

NOW REASON'S DROWNED...

Now Reason's drowned
Amid a flood of fools fearing fools,
And folly's crowned
With witless words, our witless minds to rule

AGAINST THE ACADEMIC

I write poems like water.
God knows what they say.
I am writing with my body.
This is writing an old way.
My eye is back to blue,
My tongue is violet-red.
Who will read this
As it is meant to be read?
I do not care.
It only matters that I dare.

THRICE THREE MAKES NINE...

Thrice three makes nine,
Swears the sage to the blind,
The heart's ahead:
The head's behind.

NAME-DROPPING

A cute little lyric
Like you wants
A good name:
Albatross.

A DANUBE?

A Danube?
In here?
The water-closet?
Picture the drift.
It is made
As I sit on it:
Made music.
Property of Brahms,
Flow-through.
We are slowly singing in the rain
On our way back to L.A.
When extraterrestrial forces intervene.
I sit, prey
To the uninvited guest.
I think I will make it.
I think it will make me.

LUPINE

Pretty lupine,
Are you supine
Or free of fault
Beneath this tree?
Love can wander,
Lupine wonder,
Why is it
You fancy me?
Hearts go tick-tock,
Yours goes hard rock,
That is how we
Know you're true,
Pretty lupine,
Supine lupine,
I'll always trade
My love for you.

FAMILY COLLAGE

Who was supposed to come?
A rose? My red day-lily?
The blue forget-me-not?
Or the revengeful marigolds,
Those hidden warriors?
Now we'll never get to know them—
Their eyes are blind,
And their other senses
Rust to the touch that steels them.

A DRAMA OF THE PLATHIAN INTERIOR

It is there.
I thought it was.
I have just been swallowing it.
I imagine a lot
If you want.
My head still has room.
I live on the tracks
That divide two by one.
You always get the same result.
This is called mathematical knowledge.
It is green. Or is it black?
I don't know how to divide that.
I can't give anything a color.
Colors just grow.
I am blue perpetual.
You are yellow.
I shall sew a flag
Out of the two of us,
And we'll fly behind the sky
And bear our news to the void.
You and I
We'll fly,
And live behind the sky,
And no one will know why,
No: and no one will know why.

THIS SKY IS MY TURN...

This sky is my turn,
I can slay it with my tongue,
I have everybody ready to run;
Should there be a little rain,
And no medicine for the pain,
I expect to have everybody ready
To run back again.

A LIE ABOUT YOU

It's the truth:
However blue it may sound,
You have lain within the ground
These two thousand years
And slept.
What were you doing down there?
Did you dream of sex?
Or the ambition of a
Roller-coaster life,
In a politician's pocket?
This I know we can do:
We can make you
The jamboree man
Of the revolving dawn,
And you won't be crucified.

A BLUE BELLY FOR ODYSSEUS

Maybe you did give it to me.
I can't see now, but you smell
Like the lotus I lost
As a child. Now I have found
You again,
My lotus, my blue friend,
Ready to carry me to the end
Of your watery road.

IF IT DID, I WAS COLD

I shall end my days
Invisible to everyone but me
And my own gliding eyes
Which will be set free
To lead me up or down,
As the case may be.

ROSE BLIND

I want time
For a little short love,
A little love like you,
A small rose will do.

My love of the rose
Has taken my eyes,
Now I must go with my heart
As my guide.

It is not such a long way,
Whatever a rose may say.

DUPLICATE

You were there:
A bass viol played the blues,
The saxophone too,
And I, I was watching
As you grew
From green to red
And red to blue—
Blue blood to you,
My lover, love renewed.

POLITICS OR THE GREAT BIRD

So: the right wing
No speak to the left wing,
And the left wing
No speak to the right wing.

Then how do we fly?

BUCKETS OF LOVE

I am never going to be washed again.
All my body fluids flow into my pen.
My brain is liquid nitrogen.
And my heart has become a cage for playing in.

OUR ROSE POEM

It's the red rose
That tickles my ear,
And lives under
The moon's gaunt sphere,
Sounding sometimes
Like a sea-blown care,
And sometimes
Like a wind-borne tear.

A SMALL BOX

Pandora might have known,
Bearing gifts for everyone:
Black calamity in an evening coat,
Blue puce socks
And bronze ties
Speckled with liquid eyes—
I am afraid to go on.
What I see is what, in fact,
I have done:
I have a new psychological wardrobe
For everyone.

Now I can define myself
By the winter wood,
Lying silent beneath the moon,
Idealizing the freezing air.
I have been through many
Winters before this:
Do I try again? Do I dare?

THE SHY ONE

What was done
In the name of man,
I hope will not
Be done again.

The irregular times move on,
Leaving their mark on everyone:
Even a young man's quiet shame
Will not make anyone whole again.

LOVAGE

I'm a dish—
But no one is eating me.
It's the breath,
Or the fat,
Or the tongue;
My eyeballs are nice—
If you eat them,
You can look into the Amazonian smoke
And see radicals.
It's no joke.
My eyes see.
They can teach you
To see me.
Sometimes I fall apart
Into squares:
Geometry is my defense.
I put up pyramids
To hide in.
Someone does not want to die.
To me, death is like a daisy
Without mourning,
asking to be loved.
A daisy can love anyone.
And sooner or later she does.

COLD STONE

The bats will be back,
Eventually, to torture us
Because of our lack
Of shame.
It is this coolness
That makes us rue
Living high on martinis.
The ice in the glasses
Melts down.
I am cold now,
A cold stone.

WHAT WE WISH

A hill, green, blue and yellow
In the fall sun,
A house in the light and shadow
Of life, clouds overhead,
And the maples a scarlet red,
Their roots prepared for wintering,
Bluebirds gone well away,
Jays and geese and the rest
Sent south to wear out
Winter warmth, the bear
Asleep for the time being,
Squirrels hoarding their nuts,
And men hunkering down with tales
To pass the long winter nights,
As the poet passed his,
In the company of gods and heroes,
Ancestors and broils intestine,
The whole old story of the race.

HA-HA'S

Do you like me?
Have you an ear for teeth?
Do you bleat?
Can you rise like yeast?
I can smell you from here.
It's not scent, it's an oyster.
The champagne's not bad either.
I swallow from time to time.
It's inevitable.
Think!

PURE AS PAIN

Pure as pain, dry as ice,
I stalk my admirers
With a mouth full of O's,
Trying out sounds on deaf ears,
Digging in for the duration.

Amber is the color of my vowels:
Verdigris carbonates them, it props
Them up like a wheat field
After a storm.

Before long I will moult my O's,
Like William in the willows,
Or Moses in the burning bush.
Who knows? I may turn out
To be a favorite of God,
A sweet, sweet father of a tribe.

This is our chance to be wise.
Don't forbode.
Alleluias are out of bounds.

PALE APOTHECARIES

My life is my gift to you,
I play it with knives,
Whatever you see of me,
You see through my eyes.

TWO BY FOUR

Are you a vision
Split by the sight
Of opposites?
We sit on contrary sides
Of the color blue:
You dressed in black
And I without hue.
If it were up to you,
The world would be through with itself.
But I see over your head,
And quietly watch
The rising body
Of the irresistible
New pink and blue
Dawn.

GOD CAN TAKE CARE OF HIMSELF

Most would not deny
That God is high,
Some would vow
That he is low,
And some would take
The two in tow,
As though divinity
Is not partial as to place,
Time or season,
And likely not subject
To reason.
God was born, lived and died:
So it is said,
By whom? and why?
It is better
Not to know,
Or you may follow,
Out of turn,
Where God went,
And we all go.

"TITYRE, TU PATULAE RECUBANS SUB TEGMINE FAGI…"

This is the sort of fall
You want for yourself:
It appears in the river
Like a round mechanical gong.
Whatever singular stars brought you
Into this world are gone,
And the moon itself
Whispers the tide
Of the rapidly darkening
Blue and white porcelain sky.

SHADOWS OF THE EVENING

It's as though you had fallen into a dream,
Impossible to be seen,
The tardy sun of fall
Turns its late rays to you
As though you would be visible
One final time before you're gone,
Before we know you've flown
Above—it couldn't be
The other place;
God Himself would not make you
Suffer that much more.
I would imagine you back here
As the fruitful Hellebore,
Or a bluebottle or a bee,
Or a dancing circus flea.
Maybe you could even come back as me:
We could trade places,
And visit each other's relatives,
And pick up the parts of our lives
That had fallen to pieces,
And fit them together with the love of
Each to each as glue:
Bert, you are gone, but you are not gone forever,
Before anyone can prognosticate
A change in weather

Or feel a tear drop on the cheek like a feather,
You will drop in:
We know, we are waiting for you within.

—In memory of Bert Fraser,
November 8, 1998

A CERTAIN HEAVINESS ON THE TONGUE

My days continue to decline.
I am entering your emptiness.
Your gravity is about to wipe me away.

The whole world is falling down.
And we: we quarrel and have
Nothing to say.

PHASELLUS ILLE QUEM VIDETIS HOSPITES AIT FUISSE NAVIUM CELERRIMUS

I cannot write
A word tonight
The light is tired
The sounds are gone
The mind is mute
The soul could rest
The heart lies down
Upon the bed
Alone as if
It would be fed
Once or twice or more, I'd say,
But now alone,
The past a stone
That keeps us all
From moving on.
O, god of love,
I see you now,
Upon the night's
Reluctant brow,
I wish I knew
You once again,
And yet I think
I'm near the end
Of all I've ever
Seen or done,
The hearts I've lost,

The minds I've won,
What is a heart or mind to me,
If I'm alone and cannot see
Where I'm meant to go from here?
Please, God, take away this fear
That I shall never love again,
The cruelest words that I can pen.

The night has started to withdraw,
My heart begins to feel less numb,
I watch the shadows now succumb
To your true grace and our true love.

Love 2

: 2000, 2002 :

LOVE 2

Love at first sight is irretrievable.
You can see it through your life's lens
Uncritically, looking for its own
Surcease, it is so strong.
Muscle cannot rule it
Nor the mind. It runs through
All one's actions like light,
Tangible as fire.
It plays with us,
Until we cannot control anything.
It makes us feel totally alive,
As though our eyes were on fire,
Our hearts strung like so many lyres,
Cutting our senses into so many pieces
Too small to be seen or remembered,
Like glass that has shattered,
A scene of destructibility.
Can we love love?
Are we not afraid?
Do we love ourselves
As much as the other?
Is it not better to retain ourselves
In one piece and sleep
At night untroubled by desire?
Or must we always be at the window,
Looking out over the road to see
If there can be any resolution
To this appetite?

You do not know what feeling is
Until you have felt love.
It occupies the body like a friendly enemy,
It is the goal of goals,
And the end of sense,
And the beginning of everything.
Do not tell me that when I love you,
I am on the winning side.
I am your victim, and you watch
Me writhe in expectancy.
There is only one thing left
To do with me:
And that is to love me back,
And bring me down from this untutored height I crave
To the plain of obdurate reality.

ACES

The moons are perilous,
And fog surrounds the mornings.
I cry over my infidelities,
And try to repair my graces.
The necklace of time
Is made of sugar-stone
And amber. It lights
The neck slightly,
And the rift over the upper lip.
I am playing jokes
With aphrodisiacs,
And hope to win back my lovers
When the dahlia blooms,
And the sea stretches itself to my horizon.
My eyes are turbulent.
Do not place your tongue
On mine again. I cannot stand
To feel emptiness, and my ears
Ride my head like a bride
Mounted on her first night
Of marriage.
I cannot live here much longer.
My heart is going nowhere,
And my stomach turns
Without result.
Let me inside you,
And we shall see
Who can whistle.

In the dark I come alive,
And love the unsuspecting novice.
The day tortures us outside.
Inside the night, we play our trumps,
And bid on aces.

ADDRESS TO A FAILED APOCALYPSE

I am not blind to you, love,
You wear me on your sleeve
Like sensitivity or a flea mating.

You prop me up like an easel
And paint all over my face
To explain me. You kill

My mystery. My features
Are supposed to speak for themselves,
But you will not let them.

I am not sprung like a watch,
I do not eat candy bars,
Desserts smell to me of rancid cheese.

I am not your Trinidad,
You cannot pull a Tobago on me.
I am no empty bundle of wind.

I am superficial, foolish, beautiful and vain,
And like everyone else, I eat pain.

A SHORT PRESENT

Who's the dam?
I could marry her
For use domestic
Or intercontinental.
She'd be a blast furnace
Ripping across Europe,
Frying tongues and
Opening up bladders
For inspection.
I love her traits —
Blue teeth and magenta
Lips, hair
Spilt by the breeze
Of her speaking breath:
I cannot tell
What will become of us,
But my wonder
Increases, impertinent, day by day.

— for Alma Guinness

IT DOESN'T PAY TO GO TO PRINCETON ANYMORE

Mama, I'm firing you.
You believe me, Mama,
When I'm laughing.
I am lying on top of you,
Waiting for an erection
To bring us together.
But love is out of the question.
It fell down last year.
I have stopped mating.
I want my own mama.
A toy with big breasts, and
A fanny worthy of you.
You are sliding around
The calendar now trying to change
The moon.
That is difficult.
The Heavens move at their own accord.
Please, Mama, turn them around.
Turn me around so I can see them.
After all, what am I without Heaven?
I think I have no future, Mama.
I must economize on my emotions.
Mama, pay me, pay me one more time,
And I will die at your feet temporarily.

OCEAN AGONISTES

Sex onomotopoeia.
Same sounds, different sex.
Can you avoid the guilt
Of associates?
Treat it like disinfection:
Sever the words faithfully
Following the current
Of your thought.

You have lived your life
In the water without a sound,
Come near us now,
It is time to spit the ocean
Out of your mouth
Before you drown.

SAPPHO

Sappho was happy:
She had love
And little girls.
I am a big man,
And keep my Sappho happy.
She is a big man,
Like me, and loves no one.

MAIDENHAIR

New houses for old:
Snails can change abode drastically.
So can we,
If our eyes can cut the sky at night,
When we are not alone.
I would choose to be a wood-sprite
Living in soldier-moss
Or maidenhair,
The rare fern meant to crown
A loving pair.
I am a forest poet,
My parentage illegitimate.
One day I will be born anew,
And remember on pain of discontinuity,
To confine my loving exclusively to you.

POSSIBLE TÊTE-À-TÊTE

I love you occasionally, when you answer
My calls, though I cannot think of anything
To say, your brain is so beautiful.
So I listen to the machine give me its message,
Then I shed bullets one more time,
Hoping my savage reaction will protect me
From your indifference.
As I say, I love you occasionally,
But those times are becoming fewer
As I grow old: I do not have time
To waste over a dead heart, an empty
Person. No time.
Maybe this poem will win a prize,
And I can name it after you,
So everyone will find out what I think of you
And me. But I have better uses for it.
This is a small poem, but then it
Has not been planned beforehand,
And it is no trap, it is not even a
Work of art. I guess I should apologize
For being churlish.
Ted Hughes died today.
Encourage me, and I can follow him
And Sylvia.
They were family.

A DREAM

It's not my favorite one,
But it isn't nugatory;
It is a sweet dream,
And adds labor to labor
Of love, exercising the joints
Of the brain that even carnivores
Would not eat. Sweet dreams,
I fall into you without hesitation.
I never know what you will offer me,
And when I find out,
I hate the answer to my question.
I fight to see what I have seen,
But it's no use. The eyes are
Closed when I see the most.
I will never know
Who I am.
My brain is operating
Like a wailing baby.
It speaks indiscriminately,
Hiding its meaning.
But what baby is not saying something?
It, too, lives in a dream,
And one day will grow
Into reality.
I challenge you now:
Interpret me, forget yourself,
And make my life's meaning your goal.

I would wish to know
Where you come from,
Who you are,
And where you intend to make me go.

THERE WE GO

There we go, into the night
Of our desires,
Carrying love along
Until it cannot see us any more,
Still quiet in the quiet heart
That we cease to hear
In the novel sphere
That we are entering.
Life has its vicissitudes,
The greatest is death,
So little understood
Even by the dying.
A lily cannot sing its praises,
Nor a marigold imitate
Its scent, love cannot
Provide a bower,
And the sunflowers see entire
Neither inside or out;
I cannot watch you go by here
And leave me wandering with the nightingale.
My body is pricked all over,
And I have nothing to show for it.
Only your memory
Guides me by the perils
Of peace and war.
Neither can keep you alive.
Neither can help me remember you
As you are.

My spring without you
Is no spring.
The jonquils don't arrive
And the tulips say goodbye.
The azaleas rout the rhododendrons.
Only plucked pink survives.
Red is closer to my eyes,
And I love the iris more every day.
What is my way now
Of loving you? To praise you
To anybody, to trust what I have known,
And to find in my life
Love's light crown.

THE KISS

Experience importunes my heart.
I push the pen across the page,
And I see love everywhere,
A rash supposition.
It is a blank love,
What you can buy
Or trade.
An accident may get you back
On the road to understanding.
I yell at myself
When I wake up.
Loss of faith
Brings an empty memory.
I have learned to project
A false disposition.
It must be my reputation
That makes me so unsuccessful,
Certainly not my exterior.
I have suitors.
I want one, but he has not yet
Stepped forward.
How will I know him?
He will kiss my ear,
And breathe against my neck,
And use his hands to caress
Me. And he will say
Something fanciful
To make music for me.

I wait for that one note,
Without knowing that
It will come.
Love is a mystery,
And its advent hidden
In nature.

NIGHTCAP

Try night on for size.
It does not fit me anymore.
I have been an expert at it.
I could eat in the dark
And find my mouth.
My ears wore silence lightly,
And my skin was accustomed
To dressing warmly.
The night is a large place.
I could kill it if I wished.
Even in the summer
You will find cold stars
In the sky, some of them lost,
And wondering where they are.
I could eat them.
They are like you,
Only you are further away from me
Than they are.
I cry with them on our sad feet
And my chest shakes with pain.
I cannot think of you
Because of you.
I trusted your desire.
You were my mind's friend.
Our beginning is barely finished.
Turn your life down and note its end.
I used to view you horizontally.

Now the bed is bare.
I am cleaning the sheets,
But my nose can tell you are still there.
Active or passive, we could trade places,
Our bodies were kin.
Both were suited to both of us for living in.
Now you abandon yourself as well as me,
And that is something I feel, but you do not see.

TERMINAL

If you can come,
Make it prurient,
And you will have an audience
And money.
You can support yourself
On your member,
Remember nothing,
And move into the future
Without any baggage.
I am holding your bags
For you because I love you.
I treat you like a glove
To keep me warm,
But we get old.
I am looking into the mirror
And see your face
And horrify myself.
I am losing my teeth
And whistle when I speak.
The ages are coming down upon us.
We are no longer wrinkle-free.
I know why you alarm me.
We will never have lived enough together.
I can still gauge you inside,
And I wonder whether
In the next life
We will recognize each other.

TO HIS LOVE

The chair crashes into the wood;
It is made of fire
And fiber optic wire,
To carry light and light's messages
Around your seat and through
Your arms. We are almost finished
By this scene: a pyre of birch
And paper leaves is rising
Around you, and all you do
Is say good-bye.
You deny that I am your friend,
That blood is red for a reason,
That the heart can be abused
And yet not stop beating
Or looking for a further love.
I feel you, I see you in pain
And try to save you so you can again
Live with me or another:
I will always have to wonder
What I did not do if I lost you.
The garden of our appetites is wide,
We browse around the flowers every day
And pluck petals before they fly away
And fall in some other place
Forbidden to us.
So you abandon me.
For me you become a dream,
And I am left to see you at night above my head

When you walk between the stars.
I look for your upward path,
And when I find it,
I hope that I, too,
Will have the right to pass.

BLUE ROTATION

Wailing. The blue mountain accompanies
The shining path of a baby in transit to—
Lilies grow in the desert ears of the Sphinx,
And tires roll alongside a dead Citroen,
A cortege.
Take me down with you. I shall serve
As supreme violinist to the orchestra
Of our history. We are falling
Off the edge of our doom,
And we lick our lips and expect
A visit. Who is coming?
Our own suffering.
Don't anticipate the rock.
Eternity will grind that one down, too.
And leave you in the company
Of its daughter: I love water. Love is a consequent
Blast here, and we avoid it after the third
Attempt to be intimate with someone straight.
My picture is slightly absurd,
But there are no questions:
My heart has not survived.
I bleed internally, and
Every idea in my head
Is floating out my ears
So I can't think. I drink
My pain in small glasses,
And cannot see beyond my nose.
I am a philosopher of the rose.

Something good might happen to me yet.
I am waiting,
It is waiting,
And the world revolves
Around no one,
Not even God.

COLLEGIUM VITAE

Only fools love themselves,
And the poet, only fools;
He thinks he deserves a small god
And waits for one,
But no one comes,
The light lengthens,
And one day it goes out,
And verse flies up to Heaven
To keep God company
And the poet out.

MOTHER'S DAY, 2000

I'll wash them.
I'll put them in reverse,
So that they can see behind themselves
And revise themselves
As their history deserves.
They live in a wide desert
Surrounded by a sea
With nothing in it,
Not even air,
Only emptiness,
Like the sea in their heads,
And elsewhere.
A whole existence would be better,
But we do not tell others how to live
Or die, we don't even answer
Their question why,
Because they do not ask it.
Pleasure is their pain,
And their pain, pleasure.
It is hard to wander away from that,
The story keeps repeating itself.
I would write even more about them,
But they will not read.
They cannot see the dark,
Or me. I am flying above them,
Having escaped the arc of their descent.
It is holy, this trajectory,
But they don't see that, either,

They just float down as though
They couldn't use their wings,
And then they pay attention to other things
That are not worthy of them.

WOE

The round nose
Twitches like a bat's slick wings,
Each eye mirthful
With whiskers trembling
On the verge of food,
Crumbs of loyalty once prized,
Now idolized beyond measure.
My pleasure is yours,
Your pleasure mine,
We travel in a circle of desire,
Moving above the head of time.
We shall be lovers for eternity,
If we live,
But should we die,
We shall leave our history behind,
Where kings and princes and the middling classes
Can all be tricked into believing
That we were happy while we lasted
When we were not.
We abandoned ourselves
Each to each,
And there was nothing to hold
Either solid by himself.
Our well of love was not very deep,
It only seemed so,
And we were at the bottom
In the dark, trying to touch
Each other. But we could not see,

Pain came easily,
And finally the end of affection,
And all we wanted
Was to get out,
But we could not.
Now we are gone above separately,
And leave behind
A story of unwary love
Retailed posthumously.

I NEED THE REST

It is one o'clock and I am tired.
I am too tired to write a poem,
And yet I write,
Because I think of you:
Of you and the fragrance of your hair,
Your turns of phrase
And purple lips,
Sweet kisses on my ear,
Your traveling voice,
And a heart that I can hear.
I hear your heart
Beat inside me,
And I wonder what I have caught.
Perhaps I am overwrought—
Or just in love.
That would explain almost anything,
Except how I got here,
And what you will do with me.
I have plenty of heart
To share with you,
And plenty of soul, too;
I am full of everything but you,
Because I wonder,
Do you love me?
Or am I alone in this Universe?
And if you say you do,
How can I believe you?

One day our love will fall apart,
And my heart will wear a bandage
Like a sign: "Do not travel here—
This is tragic ground,"
And I give it to the whole world to see
What love can do to anyone and me.

THE EAR-RING

She will just have to wait for her dinner:
The eyes on her frontier are bland,
And her breath obnoxious,
Her tongue a little lazy
And tart in delivery.
Who puts love into this machine?
Where does the blood go
That operates these vessels?
I would try to lie
Beneath her if I could,
But she is protected like a President,
And the closest I can get
Is to hear her recite
The litany of recalcitrants
Who do her wrong.
She is long.
Is there truth in all these syllables?
Does litotes appear?
Is one oxymoron dating another?
Or do words play not with us but with her?
I am with you:
We must tell her
Why we are here
Hanging on her ears
Like two tear-drops
Or plastic pearls—girls wear the jewelry
In this house to express their power,
And we fear to feel them

Above us and under foot
At the same time.
I am not wearing white tie—
I am no conductor or pianist,
And I am ready to be
Anyone's audience,
If only this feminine
Devil could decide
What she wants from me.

THE HEART'S GRACES

Commit to love,
And you have committed to everything,
A ring and wedding-skirt,
A veil to hide the face
And lace to hide the rest.
You are the painter
Of a list of graces,
A joint smile and liquid kisses,
A little lisp when nervous,
Wondering where your blood will go,
Or where the seeds of love will fall;
Wondering whether your heart will ever
Be deceived, and if you have chosen well
The first time in love—
Not by force but by choice,
Nor for money or for station,
But your whole being's intimation
That this was the right spouse
When you met him,
And still is.
He, no fool, can supply above love
The will that will bring you together
Whenever the sky stops shining
Blue and other couples start pining
For their past.
He carries his future
And yours like a lantern,
He has talent for beating chance

Taking your future in his hands
Until the ultimate sun sets
And he has won every bet
Anyone ever placed on you;
You are the blue truth,
The epitome of love without rue,
The guaranteed memory
Living through all ages
As dean of principle:
Together you move more than one,
And more than one moves you.

—For Gordon and Kitty Stanton

SAVED BENEATH THE SEASON

Look toward the moon:
Rain is falling from it like the dew.
It lands on blue,
And it drips curtains
From its fingers
Like bearded moss lost in antiquity.
The Age looks like the moon:
Pocked, it wears itself like snow
Or travertine,
Pitted marble from the quarry of the heart,
No new vibrations here,
Only the color of red sere
Marking our birth,
Hearing with love's ear.
We run, but we find only our singular
History at the closing of the track.
Some would turn back if allowed,
But time is unified
And cannot crawl back to where it began.
It can only say
What day it is,
And where we are in it.
Drink your tea, and you will know
As much as time does.
The sun's red teeth bite true,
And will not burn out soon,
Unlike you or me,
Doubled in sophistry.

I am waiting for myself behind you,
Waiting for the season's decrees,
Waiting for you to please me,
Ready to come up soon
Behind our fate, out of the water
And into the fall.
We take a risk,
Choose love's ambiguity,
And win the biggest wager of all.

A COLD COMPLAINT

The simplest script
Is what you write
On the prison door.
Your brain is being constantly closed
By you predilections,
And you don't mind.
My mind is constituted differently:
It takes place on a table,
And screams when the knife cuts.
Your knife will settle into me
In the long hours
When I am asleep
And can do nothing.
You pick at me,
You make my sides ache.
My body is a pool of pain,
And my brain is wrapped
Around a blaze that will never go out.
I am lost to fire,
My skull is carbonized,
And my skin dries
More quickly than a sail
In the summer sun.
One day my soul will be red,
My lungs black without breath
And my heart blue.
One day I will turn into you
And find death a delivery.

My gift will never have been taken,
And the world poorer than me
For its loss.
Some day soon I shall exit this life
And try another station somewhere else.
The seas will weep,
The trees will wallow
In the fog and mud,
Time will turn itself
Over on its back,
And heave one final syllable
Into the void.
Love, it will cry, love
Has brought us to this,
How unconscionable!

THE RUE POEM

Go on, sit down and write it.
Put your head in your lap
And prove to me you're not a man.
I can wish you into eternity,
Or give you a broom
And make you love's janitor.
The circle of your misdeeds is widening,
And the color will fall from your history
And rot before you can define yourself.
I am tired of your delusions,
Your sycophancies and your prescriptions.
What you want, you want for yourself,
Your generosity is like fruit dried
On the vine; there is little there to eat
Beyond seeds, and once they are eaten
They do not make babies.
I wonder how to get rid of you,
But you will not look into my eyes,
So I cannot see you.
The husk defeats me,
Your clothes are rampant travesties,
And the size of your malefactions is still unknown.
One day I will put you in my pot
And cook you, and then the world
Will be free of its chains for the first time
Since I came to you. You have fooled me
For many years, and I have thought the prize
You offered me was worthwhile and true,

But it is not, and you, love, you,
Are dangerous beyond measure
Until we can sort out our seed
And find some way
To plant ourselves differently,
Then we adjust truthfully to each other.

WEDNESDAY'S TREASURES

The feedback is back,
And the words dine on worms
Imported from the pains of success,
Where the truth is excess,
And men swear by politics.
Your two frightened arms can drag you by
The entrance to your own life.
Some people never go in that door,
And it is cold outside.
I wonder where warmth is
In the winter, and take my time
Standing like an egret
Amid the dying pines.
Snow falls on my hair,
Spectacles blind me,
And my ears droop.
I have hung a ring in my nose,
And it smells faintly of blood.
I am laughing at my own birth and death,
There is so little between them.
One day I will turn around
And find you at my back,
Looking for me.
Love can hide in ambiguity,
Or is it indecision?
I would like to know you
And make my fate secure.
I would like to make lilies die for me.

Then you could tell my history
To everyone. Love is not leaning on you;
The pulse is still there, your atmosphere
Is my darling. I breathe you in and out,
And see how sweet you are.
Your eyes are blue enough to kill,
And one day they will,
And I shall move beyond the circle
Of what you have made unforgivable.

A PRAGMATIC IDEAL

I will put you on the little side of laughing
If you tickle me.
I fly into ecstasy every time
You move into my sight,
I think you are so handsome.
Do not adjust yourself:
I love your thighs slightly open,
Your muscular arms at your sides,
Your neck bent slightly back
Away from your brown hair
That falls over your forehead.
When I look at you inside,
I am filled with my own lips' exhalations.
I slip at the edge of fantasy.
When will you turn to look at me?
Are you blind, or only half-alone?
I am afraid you do not trust me,
Or will cast a plague upon me,
Or overlook me in the crowd we call renowned.
One day your legs will move against mine,
And I shall ascend into the sky with my idea of you.
Heaven knows I deserve you,
But then, I do not deserve Heaven;
So I shall lose you
To one more ripely shaped,
More well attuned to your modesty,
Your quietly yielding heart,
And the sweet and bitter touch of your love's honesty.

ODE

My day is poison
Beyond redemption.
The clouds are brown,
The blue sea eclipsed,
The starlings black in masses
By the moon.
At night you can hear the loons
Moving, rising on the summer swell,
Fanning over me;
Do I dare see this movement,
Move this harmony?
I am again afraid
Of falling.
I wish the day would open over me
And Aeolus direct his bursting cheeks my way,
And give me breath.
I lie a bit to the right of death,
The devil will pierce me with his tail;
I am a little sad for myself.
I might have saved a soul,
Or led a heart to happiness,
Or shown an ill mind
How to unwind the fabric of it pains.
I cannot gain anything
From thought for a morrow
That does not exist.
I am lost in my own thoughts
Of fanciful vacancy.

Keep your lips away:
They can no longer cure me.
Even my art is gone.
I have no hope,
No expectation that there will be any more dawns
For me. Nothing calls my name.
I call it back,
And wish that it would take away my pain.

TIME IS FALLING DOWN

Kirilenko: fire the innocent
And retry the bomb.
I will fall out of it
Some day and gas
The masses lined up
Behind aggression.
I cannot stand self-aggrandizement.
Get off me!
Or you will be separated
From yourself.
The rest of you
Bears no mention.
I am only a knee
Or two in you.
It has come to this—
You are reduced to your joints,
And they are failing.
Do you get a C for deportment?
And F for verity?
I am looking straight at your groin:
Life can be empty.
We try to remake ourselves in our offspring,
But they go away.
I suppose I would like to live.
I am red inside.
Love screams at me sometimes.
I wait for it to go by.
Then I make a move
And lose everything.

THE PRESENT

Wellspring of the mind, dilute me.
I am walloping pots,
And candles light my way.
The dark is crushing me
As bats fly by the fires
We have lit to see them.
They keep us company
At dusk, and retreat
At a hint of sun.
The light is there,
And they are not,
They are creatures
That cannot live
To see themselves.
Do we see ourselves similarly?
Does the tide of dark
Take away one ounce of life?
Is the night blue,
Or is it black?
What size star
Fits our sight?
Is anything at night golden?
Or is that color
Saved only for the day?
Amber we can see.
But lust is the color we call lovely,
And we can't see it.
Babies are born into perpetuity,

But they are made in the shadows
Of obliquity.
They are the sometimes welcome
Present we give ourselves, and
The giving can be keen,
But the present is not always
The gift that it would seem.

REGINA IS THE FAULT

Regina is the fault.
Elasticity is her revelation.
Scope is accessible,
But you have to move right,
Or the devil's tail will hang you.
I am looking at the eyes of the zebra,
They counter legend
And roll across the sky
Like the plain,
Filling life up again
With its own toil,
Wondering where to go
In the midst of pain,
The same hoof hobbled by light
And age, a chronic sore
That runs a corner round white.
I will show you my strength in fall
If you desire it.
You are up to my knees in artificiality
But you haven't got them down yet.
I am still playing with you.
You are serious and I am a toy.
The land levels with me sometimes,
And I know where to find you.
Lilies grace your lips,
And the hill's brow
Turns snow aside in the spring
And makes meal of the winter.

I am inside you now,
And I feel the heat distilled
By your blood moving me
Deeper and deeper into you.
God grant me another life
And I will die twice.
The interim is without remorse.

BLASTING

Here we go, behind the blithe pragmatism,
Blushing tears down cheeks in unison.
I am the size of silence.
I adumbrate myself.
The millennium to come adores me.
I speak to the future like a friend
I have been sparing for a long time—
He is mine now, and you haven't a clue.
If you don't put him down,
I'll shoot you with my surprise.
You'll fall into disuse
Because of this.
Anyway, you lie too much,
Even with actions.
Movements can move the wrong way.
I eat a non-linear peach or plum,
Or a potato on my fire.
The scum abound around me.
They posture, but I know their aliases,
And one day I shall bring them all
Out into the open,
So that they can see me for the first time.
I do not love them very much.
It is too heavy, all this passion
And compromise.
Yes, the liars are still there,
And I am wringing their locks
To see what I can find
Underneath their empty
Attractive heads.

BABIES

Who is bailing out of the drink?
Is action active?
Do words cogitate?
I am imbibing you
Like cotton candy
Melted at the fair.
You are not all there,
But I love you,
Subordinate as you are.
Are we traveling up the right road
To the after-life, or are we
Sitting beneath palm trees
Waiting for coconuts to fall?
I see milk in your breast
And wish to taste it:
You are my baby,
And I am yours.
I promise you everything
We see in ourselves. Loving babies is alacrity
Without braces. Suspend
Your judgment a moment
And you will see: babies
Are everywhere.
I am running short on my own baby.
She is billowy
And loves the wind like a good sail.
It may blow her away
Through the trees

And other natural obstacles,
But I always find her
Where we began:
Inside the idiom of babies,
The lamb on the highway,
The loving iamb.

DOUBLES

I am popping about
Like a hot corn on ice.
Has my heart been served up cold?
Are my haunches alive for rotting?
Time is away,
And I count my fingers slightly,
Wondering how I can get past ten.
I walk on my toes,
But I cannot feel them.
They are too far away
For me to see,
And I tickle no one.
(The shrimp are still at sea)
I am dining beneath
My colleagues.
They sing better than me,
So I am leaving.
There is one who would help
If I slept with him,
But I abhor triangles.
Still, sex pleases me.
I turn up at night,
Ready to go to bed,
And walk away, unattached.
The story is continuing,
With a different ending every day.
Soon there will be an explosion,
And everyone animate

Will hear the blast.
I will be at ground zero.
Some have waited for this
All their existence,
And never found it.

BOUNCE

OK. We'll watch the watch carefully.
At last the sky falls
Beneath our toes.
The horn fixates on fast forward,
My tape rules tennis out,
St. Vitus roams along Lethe,
Bellowing like a new pupil,
And the rich go to a dance
In the swamp just outside Pensacola.
My mouche is kissing me on the lips,
But I swat it successfully
Because I am beyond being tickled.
My role comes in to roost
Over my head, and my death
Is no longer armed.
Starvation was not in the line-up,
But the pain was great, and
Leading up only to one thing.
I was being prepared by the chef-de-cuisine,
Whose name I never knew.
Anon. kills Anon.
Is this news? Not if it is anon.
I know one well-travelled hippopotamus.
He has been a good businessman.
The bad ones eventually appear before you naked,
And you can fire them once it is too late.
Death levels the playing field pretty dramatically.
I was there, but I never noticed.

Now I can see what I missed.
I wasn't much in my heyday,
But I could have abused an eye or two.
Now I am falling all over
As I anticipate one kiss.
The stars float somewhere,
We eat a joint of lamb for dinner,
Someone is singing out the evening,
We drink champagne.
There are things to do no one ever thought of,
And we should find out what they are.
We are all looking for the same thing:
And that is our way out.
Can you really count the stars
And not believe in God?
I wear the ladyslipper
And can dance the jig.
Death comes to all of us,
And it goes, too.

WHAT DO YOU REMEMBER?

I am crying over my incompetence.
My love eludes me,
My eyes see a blank wall,
And my feet step onto themselves,
So that I cannot walk.
I walk in my mind,
I talk in my mind,
But there is no effect.
My brains are bubbling with anticipation,
But creation is not theirs.
I wish I could forget my past—
My pains and my wherewithals.
I have nothing without love,
I am a mysterious ship
Beating the sea.
I cannot fly by the waves,
Or hear the tramp steamer
As it comes down upon me.
I am not unique,
But I am not the same.
I am like no one I know,
Only there is more here than I can admit.
Damnation follows me around like a dog.
I lost my insides, and I am dinner
For a party of one.
I cannibalize myself.
I think I am a delicacy
Of brown and white,

Granular but wholesome,
With a few bones and some emotional barricades
Built in. I do not know
How to preserve what is left of me.
Perhaps sea-brine, like Nelson's—
A tun for a victim.
I am my own victim.
I ride on the sky
Every day, and yet I cannot find
The one, only one, that will love me.
I am growing old backwards;
I disdain my past.
I am planted like an oak
To travel solidly through time.
One day I will find you
At the edge of my compass,
And one day your heart will find mine.

PROLEGOMENA TO ANY FUTURE METAPHYSIC

I frighten myself,
Living at the edge of dexterity.
My right hand is impoverished
And will not join the game
Of handling money and desire.
On the left we have a secret quantity
That will appear when it is required.
I do not foresee any delinquency
On the part of either, as long as
Illness does not require a handicap
In the middle of the contest
Between one state and another.
We go off this way,
And find ourselves new beings
To play in like comedians,
Trying to shadow the past
With a new incarnation.
Maybe we will find love this time,
At least something like it
That will not knock us down
In private.
There is blood here at risk
And two more deaths
To be calculated.
The end is not obvious.
I cannot tell you what my eyes
Give to me when they see you

Successfully. I do it again and again,
And hear you with blatant ears,
Wondering where all that sound
Can be coming from.
A great man comes marching down
My mind to be with you,
He has anointed me, and made me
A part of him.
The only thing left to show
Is where the sun flies,
The star lies, and the moon
Sows. Then there can be no mistake
About who we are, where we're from,
Or what everyone is free to know.

HOW WE END UP

There is no way to get around me;
I am your love-foe,
And you will not move
Until I let you love me.
I kiss your empty lips
And your wandering velvet hair;
I make a purse of what I do not owe
But bestow upon you freely.

I will never be out of love: if it is not you,
Then I shall find your brother
Somewhere in space,
Billowing for an hour or two.
That is my power, and it shows
I can have anyone, but I am now with you.

I wonder whether you have felt me,
Or whether I am posturing like an amateur.
Love is a bitch that barks blindly
Into the dark, leaving us to fall over
Where we are.
I see you, but I do not see you.
You are silent,
And say what I do not want to hear.
The cranes are flying above me,
And the hoopoes make a big noise.
I am lost in birds,
I cannot fly,
And my ears are full of assignations.

What will you do to my reputation?

I begin to think love is a contradiction in terms.
I fear it more than death's own symbols.
It makes me talk to myself,
And beseech the lilies
Not to look at me.
Where does this pain take us?
What is the grief it gives us?
Can it become our incubus,
An engine of defeat?

TIME IN

If you want to cash me in,
Remember, I am outwardly mobile:
My mind flies in the dark
To pinnacles of perceptive expression.
My heart still shakes drastically,
Until I drink it like coffee or tea,
Although I always thought it was an ice.
Now it burns my tongue,
And makes my nose run
All the way past my misogyny—
Even Sappho refrains from
Laughing at me.
She wants the girls that flock to me,
So she is polite,
And refrains from mocking anyone
With her poetry.
I do not need Sappho to teach me anything,
Life is deed,
And nothing comes of nothing
Save what's empty.

It is early in the morning,
And I have awakened to a new perplexity—
I cannot love myself to death any more.
I am no longer my own creature.
Pain does not disable me.
My head has cleared,
My mind is not full of spikes.

And my body is functioning like fire,
Independent of my past.
I celebrate: I am new, no longer old,
And cannot find my own shadow to walk in any more.
I even survive the absence of love, since I now know
That one day it will come to me sooner than before.

WAITING/REPULSED

I don't know.
I take a fall in the spring
And never get to the summer.
I live upside down,
Proposing pleasure where there is none.
The live anticipate me,
And I wander like a worrisome little soul
Into the dark of my being.
I wish I could come out,
But the dark is undeniable.
I touch it slowly,
And it takes me into places
Rich to me.
I distinctly hear
The cries of other abandoned souls,
And wonder what their pain is like,
Whom they loved that betrayed them,
And where they have gone
To find solace.
Madness is black, too,
And cannot save you.
Who has the handle on that?
I love everyone the wrong way.
My love is green as spring,
But not so beautiful.
I wish I knew a beauty.
I wish a beauty knew me.
I wish a lot of things,

But I am beginning to think
Perhaps they will kill me.
There are many mysteries,
And I am only one.
Every day I drown,
Then I dry my hair,
Listen to my skin crack,
And continue.

HIDING LIGHT

My survival is without bounds.
It spills over into your universe,
Breaking the limits of love
And notoriety. I have a
Reputation for ambiguity,
And its extravagance drives me
As I try to practice self-control.
I leave the match
Thinking all is won,
But there are other people in the world,
And, like little crabs, they hang on to me.
I fight back,
And the black one is my victim.
It is his own actions
That bring him to it.
Watch the purge,
And you will learn something.
The grass has turned green in the rain,
And we see for ourselves
The east shore of the rising sun.
Words carry their full meaning.
The North becomes South,
And the South, North.
Life is no longer limited
To three dimensions outside of time.

One day my heart will travel to you
So fast that you will never know it.

My love is a whisper in the dark,
A shadow of warmth beside your breath.
You are mine and not mine:
I refuse to steal your self away from you,
Despite my inclination.
I love you so much,
Courtesy carries forgiveness—
The word is out, the word is trust,
And I come with it.

A VISION

The brain plays fitfully
With me. I am lost in
My body, and try to think
Myself out of my dilemma.
Lobes protrude from my ears
Until I resemble a bird with big wings.
My mirror shocks me,
I see web feet,
And I grow plates
Out of my tongue.
If I turn around
To see where I have been,
I can only see where I am going.
I am becoming
A gentle being, enough
Monster to intrigue children
And make adaptation critical.
I remain lively,
And move slowly enough
To whisper sad words
Out of my distorted lips.
I have a message for everyone:
Fight me out of fright
And you will lose.
Accept my nakedness
And we can work together
To make our world
Strong in unison.

I never thought it would take this sacrifice
To make us univocal,
But it does not matter.
The goal remains the same
As it ever was with me:
A happy life for everyone,
And everyone at peace and free.

SOUTHAMPTON

Kill my dog
Or kill myself.
Whose blood runs
Beneath the surface
Of our enmity?
I will set you out to dry
Like sauce that lies
In my dead lap.
You eat me carefully
To avoid spillage.
But my love falls anyway,
As your mouth soaks me dry.
I am half Jew,
Half blue-blood,
And I have slit my eyes
Into crescent moons,
Like Asiatic fans.
Life cries
At the side of pain.
I would move toward the truth,
But for the reception I await.
I feel too much,
And honesty proves no gain.
I make allowances for courage,
And end up alone.
Toss me a bone,
Fate: you are too heavy,
And there is nothing I could have done
To avoid you.

PERIANDROS

The lively amputee
Wings it successfully
Toward eternity.
He converts disability
Into brain cells,
And lights up his mind
And outer climes
To the mystery
Of persistent life.
His eyes are turning white with age.
Macular disease will blind him one day.
But he will still see
The truth about things.
There is an inner light in pain,
A second or third sight
That tells us how
To go in the dark.
The ark was in the main,
But did not sink.
Shakespeare fell in love
More than once,
But never shrank from fate.
The purity of fire
Helped him,
And the salvation of desire.
Did he end disconsolate,
Or wise in abnegation?

The truth is, he told his own story
More than once,
But we have yet to see
It.

PRETTY PIKE

We'll be there soon.
I eat left, you eat right,
Our quarry, hunger, cannot escape us.
We are being blown apart
Like spinnakers in a stiff wind.
I am still eating left,
You have left the right
To eat me.
What a hazard all this can be,
A seaside banquet for the mailmen.
Do we look for hazard in a bad diet?
Is it all we have left
To know each other by?
Our identity is inside us,
But I feel it leaking out.
We are swimming on the red tide,
The sea floats by,
And time is black.
I cannot watch myself now,
Though there is a faint phosphorescence
Around you.
Someone is blessed,
And you say hello.
Our backs are turned, and a child
Is singing of Christmas.
It is your song,
Accept it.

I have been south before,
And I know what to expect.
The shoes fit,
And the trail follows the tune
Into the hollow.

GOODBYE, DOG

I am waiting for my shadow
To catch up with me,
So that I may leash it to kill
My love for you.
You taste of dark places,
And bedevil the red orange
And the black apple.
Your fruit is rancid
As old fat,
And my nose notices
The end of something rotten:
Your foreign fur
Or a mildewed handkerchief.
Your fumes drive me away,
And I watch my shadow grow
As it succumbs
To my intestinal disjunctions.
The fish I once caught is withering on the stick,
And the stones beneath my toes
Cut me on the shore.
The cold inside
Blinds my inner eye,
Once fragrantly in love.
Your eyes remain two,
But cannot see within me
Or outside you.

THE PILOT

I will turn you in
If your life is inexpensive.
I call you garbage.
Your cabbage is cooking
In my nose,
And your ear
Is distant.
Our illumination is getting dense,
And as it moves,
Fremantle sees the end of his troubles.
I have never met him,
And he knows who I am.
As I wander away from you,
We become closer together.
I will point you out to him
When the weather improves.
In the meantime,
Snow licks the pavement,
And salt clogs the muddy roads.
The mountain is becoming impassable,
And my stem unbreakable.
Your size unnerves me:
Can you drive me home?

EMPTY HAZARD

I think you're right:
The list of inconsistencies would do in
A philosopher, and logic would go wild
To use such a template for experience.
What you do is inexplicable,
It has no meaning in space-time,
Euclid would laugh at you,
And Spinoza would sacrifice his eyes
To see you. You misconstrue
The gift of love,
And the lack of sense you bring to it.
Why do you pale in front of me?
You do not suit:
Your eyes are too wide,
Your ears fly out,
And your mouth is not ripe for a kiss.
Your hair is indescribable,
And your breath the devil.
I have a heart that will never see yours,
Your inner workings are so impossible.
You cannot keep me from wandering.
I fall asleep at your touch, and
You do nothing successfully.
I promise myself to stay away from you,
To leave a cold trail you cannot find.
You are empty, and I look through you
Only to see an elementary mistake multiplied
By a thousand hazards.

NIGHT LIGHT

I should have painted you a long time ago.
Your sun sweeps across my magnanimity,
You are so bright in the twilight of desire.
Your legs betray you to me
And away from me.
I do not skip with you
And cannot: I am down
Where you never go.
You are the hidden sweets
Behind my dreams,
Yet you remain insubstantial
As this thin knife of life
Slicing at my skin.
You do not hurt me —
I have pulled my feelers in
And remember nothing,
Not even the length of your face
I once loved. Why do you turn to me still?
Why do I think of you at all?
Are my feelings so perplexed,
My will so far gone?
I try to love myself
As much as I loved you.
Love and pain:
Sometimes they seem so elegant
And inevitable. Sometimes
They seem a simple recipe
For the death of expectation.

Once I was on fire.
Now—now my eyes are white
All the way through,
And that is one reason I will never again
See you.

DALLIANCE

Customer expense.
I am writing on the wall.
I am reading myself
As I walk in a circle
Around my groom.
He is handsome, with yellow hair
And a smile to beat Midas'.
My man is gold,
And I provide him with his alloy.
He even loves me—unexpectedly—
Because I make him smile.
I think he is far more beautiful
Than me, and he will never despair
Over my eccentricity,
Which he loves.
I wonder, where does the truth go
When two true hearts fly apart?
One day I will find out.
My age undermines his heart and makes
Me cautious. Love is a trick
That I sometimes know how to play,
But I do not. That is not the way
To follow a warm body.
I move up and down
When I make love,
And my love does the same.

Are we to be penalized for who we are,
Where we are, and what we have always
Wanted to say?—I love one only,
He loves me, and memory will never
Let anyone forget this—no one, no way.

TRAGEDY TURNS AWAY

This is my fine paper.
I write on it to choose sides.
There is a precipice
Outside my window,
And I am clinging to it in my mind.
One day I shall reach the top,
And then I will die
Like a whale hung by a high tide
Or a lemming rushing to embrace his future.
My future is secure:
I am running toward you
And away from you.
I am above you,
And can see how you will win the race
Against me
By ducking under the ropes
That separate you and me
And giving me a kiss.
I am already out in the world:
My mind has made
My pain public.
My love for myself
Declares it so.
I am not falling down any more.
The floor of tragedy cannot find me any more.
I laugh and look into the new day.
Everything is there for me.

Even my madness has gone away
And left me tickled by fatality.
I cannot believe I am here to stay.
But I am.

War

: 2003 :

THE STORY OF MY LIFE

Please don't tell me.
I am not apparent to you.
Fidelity is seeking me,
And I withstand calumny
To find it.
I pour tea over myself
As the clean air drinks me.
My hair falls out
Upon my sloping shoulders.
I am falling into my feet.
My head is plunging
Into the ground around me.
My neck is severed,
And my arms are disarmed surreptitiously.
I am a study
Of downward consistency. My chest falls,
My waist constricts,
And my legs collapse
Like two dead trees.
My foundation, my feet,
Subside, and I
Am not anything.
This is how towers fall,
In soot and smoke,
And the pall of dead bodies.
We feel their blood congeal.
There is sovereign hate here.
It will not go for awhile.

Then, almost at the very last,
The spirit of life revives,
Where once we were forced
To burn our boats,
Now we float back upon the tide,
We move in new, flashing bodies,
And rediscover Paradise.

WHOSE HORSEMAN?

You're going to have to help me
With this one,
Because I don't know what to say.
My hair is turning white with age,
Like the birch trees
That lose their greenery in autumn,
Leaving behind their silver skin.
I once looked like a winner.
Now I wince as time ploughs
My face, my ears wane,
My eyes no longer see themselves
In my mirror.
I am still a picture of myself—
I cannot escape yet into meaning.
The sweetness of being eludes me.
Time is overwrought.
The two towers have fallen down.
Flowers fall down in fall,
But not two towers.
We do not see what we see.
We cannot escape into inevitability.
I am losing my words.
My tongue plays tricks on me.
The dust settles in my open mouth.
There are sheets everywhere,
And death lurks
Underneath the world's wreakage.
Love, wealth, honor, power

Have not saved us from this.
Can we be our enemy?
Who hates us,
That we should find our death
In the everyday?
This is not every day.
Our bodies already
Begin to putrify.
We are lost on earth—
We are the dead,
And whether anyone cares or not,
Our identity is forever secret,
Where we go cannot be found,
And we cannot be found
Except in the shroud
That drapes us all
As we pass by
Unseen into the unknown.

WAR

It's getting late.
The horn outside
Announces the impatient mind,
Blind to the block we live on,
Rigid like a rock
That does not care
For anyone, solid
In disdain.
There are soldiers in our hearts,
Our minds being martialed
To support our sons and
Weapons of vast destruction that
Go to the front lines.
Pity the enemy, if you will,
We know how to kill
Better than he.
We have harnessed technology,
Power no one has ever seen,
The ability to wage war invisibly.
This is not a trial between even hands.
One side holds clubs,
The other plans for the bright hearts of man.
Some will die,
Others lose a leg
Or eye,
Or arm or simple innocence.
Even the mind can go
If too strongly stressed.

Pain can confess pain,
And still the soul survive;
Love is fallen,
But will rise
Again, and choose for its object
All who live
One war from Paradise.

GOING UP

It's not supposed to happen like this,
I am perspiring love,
My eyes turn around in my skull,
I chew my ears so they cannot hear,
I pull my hair out in tufts,
I have every kind of cancer
And stay alive.
I live on a knife.
I do not desire my life.
I am limping into the buttercups
And wonder whether they will soothe me.
The season is near an end,
I have set aside my evening clothes.
I will never wear anything like that again.
I was a penguin once in petticoats,
Cold and unfriendly.
I tried for love.
I think it was a trial by fire.
It started, and I extinguished myself.
The burning felt like ice.
My heart was palpitating,
And I could not take it.
I am better level.
I watch my toes as I walk on the road.
The mud is soothing me.
One day I will go up
And forget all my lines
In the face of the loved one,

And then he will walk away
And leave me feeling
Preposterous.

I HAVE SAVED A LIFE

Suicide is like a life-jacket:
It saves you from yourself
Just in time: before you
Really learn how to live.
It is succulent,
And leaves disposal
Everywhere. It lies
To the world and tries
To keep its mind secret.
The professionals profess to understand it,
But they have never felt it.
It feels good, even better
If you never get anywhere.
I like to indulge myself
Sometimes by telling myself
I will die by
My own hand,
And then I annul my plan.
I put my end off to another day
And sit down to dinner.
I would rather not tell you
All about it. It is contagious,
And I am irresponsible.
Watch me, I can flame out anytime.
Even God cannot put my fire out.
I am my own property.

Lightning has struck twice
In the same place,
And I am still here.
I wish love were as capacious
As denial.

THE CHARMING FACE OF DAWN

Orange juice slides down my bib
As I wail into my mother's face
Uncontrollably. I want my fist
In her eye, she is so inflated.
I am my own potentate,
And I will only eat yams
If I approve of them myself.
I want to choose my food,
And my mother, too,
If I have to.
Parents are not irreplaceable
In my world.
I am mixing mine—
I am growing beyond control
By anybody,
And the police
Are beginning to take an interest in me.
I am not afraid.
I hide behind the birds,
And provide nests
For the sea-turtles.
Nature loves me, and I can shrink
To the size of a periwinkle.
Turn me over,
And you will find
My love upright.

Dawn is purple
Between my legs,
And my brow
Is the size
Of the horizon.

LAURELS

The night has become empty.
It is one big eye
Reflected in eternity,
A rose window
At dawn,
The peculiar scent of angularity
That travels unimpeded
To the stable out back.
I wonder who is going to ride
The horns of the terrorists.
I push death backwards,
And try to beat the enemy dead
With my own hands.
But pain outweighs me,
And I fall into the trap.
Lie to me a little.
I need a little fantasy in my life,
Something to open my eyelids
When I wake in the morning.
My fingers are freezing
And I rock on my heels
Out of genial boredom. It snows, and
Love is at the bottom of my list.
I would rather meet my fate elsewhere,
In the chambers of the day, perhaps,
Or the dome of the night.

I am right about myself:
The truth is fragrant,
And I deserve
A crown of laurels
For my pains.

COMPLAINT

I'd rather turn upside down
Than play with you.
You are pneumonia,
And you destroy me.
Under you,
I cannot do arithmetic in my head,
I cannot write my name,
And my breath comes
Shorter than my hair.
You are big enough to keep me here.
I have written all I know.
And all I can do now
Is respect myself.
And yet I hear new words,
And find new slates to see,
Love still moves me,
My ears roll open,
And my brain begins
To turn around again.
The cool is beginning to warm up.
I can see the snow slide outside,
And the sharp icicles
Threaten to fall onto our heads.
We break them off the eaves
And are safe again,
Pneumonia or not. Beyond the crisis,
We begin to exhibit all

The established symptoms.
We are beginning
To die upside down;
Does anyone care to fawn over us?
Are we going to return once
We are gone?
The news cries over us,
And we cry back,
And wish we had a voice
That could be heard.

THE TRAP

There are four nights a week
When I try my mind,
The rest of the time, I telegraph
Myself to the outside
Using my thumbs
And sometimes my tongue,
Though that is rare,
Since I must use spare
Diction and symbolic mime
To hide behind.
I speak in signs,
And leave others to judge
What I say.
My grave is without rhyme,
And I live in the kingdom
Of Paradigm. I push
My nose forward
To indicate 'knows',
And keep my hands celibate
In my pockets
Where change is loose;
My hair multiplies
Into a noose,
My heart palpitates between
Love and pain,
And my eyelids
Are red with envy.

It is the same
If I turn down my collar—
I can be a clown,
Or a soldier on the front lines
Of etiquette.
My catch is incomparably rich—
I can say everything in a single touch,
And I do,
And that is why you want me dead or alive
Before I catch you.

AMPLIFICATION

This is a biography.
This is the color of my heart;
I bleed quietly.
I am attacking the emptiness,
And finding a cure in solace.
Make me smooth here,
I am not afraid
To spit on fear.
I walk down the street
And peer into the unknown.
My eyes roll,
And my tongue bristles
At what it has to hear.
My teeth are red
From eating ice.
Someone has been feeding
Upon the dead.
All I can see is in front of me—
There is nothing normal anywhere.
I am flying in the atmosphere.
Ashes cover a dying sun,
And I think I may be called.
Love me or not,
I have to go.
My life is only a small show,
But in it I find an answer
To the cold.
There is a change in the wings:

The actors prepare for a new stage,
A new play,
New worlds,
And the death of death itself
As it unfurls.

I AM GOING

It's hot water
I swim in,
I swallow it savagely
And my ductile throat
Breathes up lozenges of
Blood-red flesh.
I am drowning
In my own body;
No one can see me do it.
The whole of me
Is paralyzed beyond endurance.
My feet are falling off,
My sex does not quicken,
My ears roll around my head
And my hair flies up
Into the stratosphere.
Where does circumstance end,
And my death begin?
Can my love for someone
Save me? Are you out there
Observing me, or am I in here
Caught in the fog?
I am trying to keep an open mind,
But my pulse is beating me
Into submission. I cannot
Feel my blood in my veins—
Am I being finally drained
Of animation? One day
I expected to die, but not now.

"I am not ready!" I shout
To the clouds; they return
The compliment—plain silence—
And I sit transfixed
By the irresistible.

LIP-SYNC

Pleasant lip-sync please.
I move with your mouth,
But we don't say anything.
The breath is not felt, but low.
The sky is in our eyes,
And they breathe blue
Through the evening.
I am crying.
My eyes flow beyond me,
And carry me to thoughts of suicide,
But you bring me back.
You say it is not time yet.
The bees have not packed it in,
The leaves are still dwindling,
The colors slowly turning brown.
It is not yet quite time to let go.
I turn around.
No one notices me.
My enemies want to stop playing with me,
But I won't let them.
They say yes once,
And can't get over it.
They throw me out with the nightsoil,
Bur they cannot get rid of my smell.
My signature is impeccable.
While they sleep,
I spend hours in the night wandering,
But I do not die,

And I do not find anything.
I provide my own requiem
At daybreak. I can hum a tune
To break the silence.
I will go up now,
Or shall I rot below?
I am food for worms
And fools,
And love no one.

THE BLUE PARROT

The cereal is turning brown
In its bowl,
And limp as the wavering
Sheets of smoke
The sun cannot penetrate.
I can put myself in you
At will, and try new
Trials to see what pleases.
You please me,
And I am not unfaithful
To my marigold,
My gilded one.
One day I might
Make a switch
Away
Out of ennui—
But now love pricks
Without mercy. Will
That god never let up?
He has his hands
Around me,
And I cannot feel anything
But his fingers
Milking me.
Or is it you I feel?
How many of us
Are there here?
Is there a spirit
Above or below?

Some thing animates us,
And it will take us
Among the roses,
All the way down
To the end of the last row.
Even age has its ears
That hear feelings.
We are due to
Love ourselves to death.
The breathing slows.
The whipporwill shows us the way to
Heaven.
We have come by here,
Green as the lawn we walk on,
And leave nothing behind
But ourselves.

LOOKING UP AN OLD FRIEND

Were you my brother
I would swing you around
To make you face me
For the first time
Since we were children.
But you are my father,
And my brother is breathing
Fast down your neck
As he tries to figure
A way to kill you
And make me mad forever.

Such is the potent
Hate of blood against blood.
I look inside myself
And find a knot
I cannot loosen.
I am anxiously waiting
To be free.
I could belong to me
Or my father or my brother:
We three are looking for a way out.

It is hard being a brother and a son.
I would like to resign
From positions of influence
And live in the jungle
With the chimpanzees.

They will give me something to eat,
And make me celibate.
Love is flying around inside me
Trying to milk
My worth out of me.
Someone loves me,
And seizes my gift
On the edge of catastrophe.
You make me plural,
And we play together in the open fields

Until we lie down tired,
Smell the honeysuckle and the rose,
Shift our toes beguilingly,
And wait to see
If ever we will walk arm in arm
Past the sheep,
The cattle and the ox-bow
On the wall;
Where did life go? I ask you,
Where did we all go?

THE TITLE OF DISCERNMENT

We'll see what we want to see.
That is the object of our reflection;
Life is a vast mirror
Of self-perception.
The eyes roll downhill
As age advances
Into blindness,
And the loss of sight
Loosens the moorings of life,
Until all that is left
Is dust or ash,
Which the wind spends.
There are other commodities
We try to save,
But time takes it all away
No matter how much
We oppose ourselves.
The body is always
A fragile temple,
And we burn within it
Temporarily.
The moor-cock calls
And we follow in the dark,
Only to become food for the raven.
We prey on peace when alive,
And ask grace for one more day
And another.
Prayer gets us nowhere.

Divinity is not here.
We ask our love
To keep us back,
Unsuccessfully.
Death is a peremptory bandit.
What we end, he begins.
We are afraid
Of everything,
And fall into our own end
Without the preparation
It deserves.
Put the pen down.
It is approaching
Silence.

I LOLL ON LILY-PADS

Plow upon the stair
Of my innermost self—
I am delving into my
Personal antiquity,
And find fossilized hope
Of all emotions
That still show the scars
I live with.
I remind myself
Of the Malthusian truth,
And wonder where birth
Is taking us
If not more death
Than we already have or need.
Marriage between coevals
Can solve some difficulties.
I lie waiting for my love
To walk up to me
And declare himself.
Love could last a little longer than life,
Then we turn around and watch
The door close behind us,
Leaving us alone and fruitless.
I pin my heart up on the wall
And listen to the wind blow it about.
I am already too late
To say goodbye,
And I do not wonder
At my tardiness.

The strength of my emotions
Must one day be complete,
And then I can choose
My own individuality
Out of my past.
I loll on lily-pads,
And wait for faith
To take me into its arms
As time fails
And I scratch my back
On the tail of the incomplete.

RECOVERING

I can't stop,
I just can't stop:
I am learning all over again
How to fix myself up,
Where to see stars
And the sea anemones
That please me in their season.
I cannot stop here:
My life was left hanging
Out to dry for many years,
But I was already dead,
And the question was not
Where to bury me,
But if—in my mind—
I could bring myself back.
And so I have survived
Into a kind of afterlife.
The windows let in the spring scents,
The breezes bend them,
The poplar whispers to the quaking aspen
That it is green,
And so am I, or almost—
My mind has its tears,
My feelings have fallen out of flux.
My doctors squint
And declare me victorious,
And I smile near the end,
As I had at the beginning.

There is esteem in my morning tea,
Sprinkled with ginger and peach.
A little arrowroot thickens me.
I am falling off my bed
Into the sea,
And I am quite sure I will live forever.

TO HIS MUSE

I have been looking
At myself in the mirror
And all I can see
Is the album of my death.
All I can see is my picture everywhere.
You have built a superstructure
Around me,
And I hear it,
But it is not me,
It is illegitimate, a blank fork
In the road I will never accept,
Having felt it once already
In the head,
A strange inward blow,
Not a good place for a tomb.
I am thirteen,
Risen into a man,
And I wash my own shirt
In my spare time.
My lawyer tells me
I haven't got much time
Left, or money,
Or happiness.
But those never did come.
I still have you,
And you have always
Shown me how to go
And under what moon,
And I thank you.

Your pleasure has been my life,
And now that I stand up for the first time again
In front of that mirror,
I see only you,
And I am sure of where I want to go
And what I want to do
With your love.

SPRING IN MAY

I am wandering through the corridors
Of my brain. Everything
Seems the same since
I last looked:
The dog in the bathroom,
The wretched mollusk
Unattended in the soap,
My purple peony,
And the final idea
To hang my life on.
Then the whole scene changes:
The firemen jump up
In blue suits
To put out the fire
Inside me, and my soul
Rises like faltering smoke over Baltic Street
As sirens blow
And red lights flash
On abandoned pillows,
Turning them red
With apprehension.
It was a sleepy spring.
Fire at night is rare.
Everyone had better
Learn how to dance on water
Without faltering,
If they want love
Beyond the catastrophe.

Love is like spring,
Only spring keeps recycling,
While love is young only once,
And we with it,
And that is a grace
To suit my faltering appetite.

IN LINE

The baby sleeps at the garage,
Brown slumber
Allowing dreams to sprout
In its head, its eyes
Quiet, watching,
Watching the purple night—
Not listening to the promises
Of the day.
There is no way to tell
From sound
What the crescent sun
Will bring into
The new strategy of lies
Men tell to their disadvantage.
Power is power,
And can often be blind
To its own true interests.
Tongues can fly through
The atmosphere to no effect,
And garlands can drape the necks
Of sometime heroes.
It makes no matter.
Alabaster and bronze
Fall down,
The dew dries,
And carcasses of dreadful sharks
Littler the outlines of our minds.

The ocean receives
Alluvial ash, and love cools,
Especially when it starts
Out hot as an ingot
Of iron or steel.
Rust comes to both,
And no word keeps
Its meaning forever:
Books die, too,
And lives go unread.
Youth is a spring that dries up
In the fall, unmeasured.
The architrave of any religion
Will not hold it up forever.
The sage
Is wary of what he knows.
We all go,
Following in inevitable line
To the shadows that hide
What we soon will recognize only
After it is useless to us.

TRAVELING LIGHT

Whose are the gags?
What has brought us to this place
Besides ourselves?
I lick myself like a dog.
The monetarism goes on,
Developing the grasp
Of an octopus
That I watch in my mind
Silently shifting.
Sea-snails lie there too.
I eat them like soft eggs
And relish the salt.
Pepper comes unannounced,
And slides genially
Down my mouth.
Then the basil whoops it up
With the thyme,
And paprika brightly lies
About revolution,
There is no solution
More voluble
Than love and tongue.
I eat some.
Then I spin away,
And look for some other
Parasite to grasp at my creation
As though it were his.
I want it back.

What I have is
What I am;
Let some politician be tall
Or a money man small and profligate.
I turn myself away
And hide behind the day
Of my death, when I knock
On the front door of all these
And find out who has bled for me.
They know I have bled for them,
And hate me for it.

NO TITLE FOR ME

I am writing like fire
On the brow of the earth,
Truth works somewhere beneath me
That I have seen before
In the clouds.
My heart is loud,
But my many loves
Do not want to hear,
My voice is too clear,
And they are used to alchemy.
So they get down on their knees
And pray,
And ask for things.

What they have
Is exactly what they have asked for.
But they cannot change
Their tune to fit my gifts.
I guess the present music
Is out of place,
But it is what I know to say.
My robes are white, not purple,
And my lips not purple but blue.
My eyes are invisible,
And my hair a glory
No one can dare to see.
I am myself,
And I am the only one,

And if you look carefully
In my direction,
You may notice a hint of real love.
That is all I can see.
And what do you give me?

THE ABLE MAN

It's not too early:
I will pick your ears
Of what you can disclose
Hidden between them,
Sitting beneath my sword.
I am a prompter at a play,
With no words,
Only geniality made substantial
By hands and feet.
I am fleet for my size,
And the gray in my brain
Moves swiftly like electricity,
Faster than yours,
Though you're not negligible.
Once I lied to you a little,
To find out what it would bring;
I began to lose track of
Who I was and everything
I stood for.
So I stopped,
And now I have you
On my tail,
Trying to perfect a masterpiece.
I crave your help,
But my life belongs to me,
Not you: my trials are numerous
And nothing new.

I am my own creation
And will continue so:
Our life together could be great,
I do not know.
And then—to say it gracefully—
I am not you.

LIGHT ME UP

It is two o'clock
And I write again.
My knees shake
And my hands have
A life of their own.
My tongue takes on tastes
I had never thought of,
But they have grown
Within me like a serpent's
Coil or the toil
Of a green-backed toad.
Love is ambidextrous tonight,
And it flies in my face
Every time I try to look at it.
I am a lunatic
Wandering through the clouds
Without worry,
Wondering where the night ends
And I can once more
Begin the day.
It is almost here,
But not yet something
I can grasp:
The truth takes you,
You cannot hold it fast.

It is a shadow just outside
The cast of your eye,
And when you look
Straight at it,
It has fled
Like a dove's wan melody.
Nothing can match
The dexterity of the light—
Hold it within,
Or you may never hold it again.

MALAISE

I do not know
What the general slant
On age is.
I am icy,
And my bonded thighs
Strangle my sex
By degrees.
My hair falls out,
And I fail to see.
Love is no relaxation,
Only an old debt
I continue to repay.
No dance moves me,
No step to right or left
Makes any difference.
No one cares what I think
Or where I play.
Time has abandoned its watch,
And love its courtesy.
I see vague fissures in my skin.
My teeth are falling in.
I cannot whistle
To the mockingbird
Nor hear the hoopoes' wing.
Good humor fades,
Society flies away,
Sweat beads where I cannot say
Or do not know.

My seed is dry,
And my ankles ache.
Who can make me over new?
Not even God has that power,
And if he does,
He uses it for someone else
At some other hour.

CONEY ISLAND

I pitch my ear
To the sound
Of Coney Island.
I watch my eye
Watch the light
Of Coney Island.
I walk along
The shore of
Coney Island and explore
The mind of time
That makes the Isle
What is was when
I was born in Coney Island.
Now I live
Beyond the limit
Of the boards
And struts and rings
That held me up
Above the swings
Of Coney Island.
I turn all colors
As I coast
Along the air
In Coney Island.

One day it may
No longer be there
As it was when I was young,
But I will always
Be young on a dare
At Coney Island.

A SONG ASIDE

The burial of the fly
Signals anticipation of the end
For other insects and animals,
Whose carcasses offer food
To the feverish larvae
Of their kind,
Lying over skin and hair
And the diseased bowels
Of the dead.
I wonder who in life
Could be so enamored of such a one
As death; who is so wretched
As to prefer waste
To holiness, and the muddy water
Of disease to streams
Of white and blue.
Where is the you
That we want to waste,
When we know that once the parting
Is done, no one comes back?
There are crooks and dark hearts,
And murderers on the lam,
Even great reputations that are clean,
And no one remembers anything
About anyone who has already
Gone. Fame cannot keep
A soul alive for long, rarely a reputation
Will suffice—Time moves through history

And consigns even the greatest
To words only the few will read
And fewer hear.
But death is near.
So look for salvation
Not in emptiness or memory,
But in the warm present,
So that we may plant a seed
Or root to the benefit of all.
Life loves itself, and rightly so,
And if it is eternal,
That is something death
Will never conquer,
And all of us shall know.

—for Andre Vernet

The Shadow Book
: 2000, 2004 :

JOHANNESBURG

i.

I have all the time there is.
No one can take it out of me.
I stand on myself
Like an hourglass.
I watch trees fall
Through an opening in time,
And know I am infinite.
I can outwit anyone.
Time yields power
Over what is finite.
Love is a sideshow,
Also pain and good fortune.
Water is low, stone durable
And fire is high.
These can all last for a while,
But the greatest of all is time.

ii.

Turn the monkey backwards.
He milks me,
And I return the compliment.
I dry myself by the basin,
And he jumps in.
It is monkey day at the workhouse.
My mind is percolating
Through his brain
And it tickles him.
He is a good friend,
And does not try
To make me count my toes.
Shoes are useless
To suit us both.
The heat is faster,
And pleasure breaks out of our foreheads.

iii.

I have been opened.
My anger is a great amnesiac.
It forgets itself
In the hottest circumstances.
I pull it in, and try
A rein or two to make it end.
The heat under the sun is growing
Until there is no shade,
No wind. We yield
To the sun, and wait for time
To rub us down.
I will lead my soul
Abroad to see
What is the price
Of all this.
I try sleeping.
It is hot.
But I am sleeping.

iv.

The doilies in my grandmother's house
Protect me. Their pins prick my hands,
But I do not bleed.
Mystery is born into mystery.
I fall into the future
Like a lame goat
And trust no one.
The past tracks me down,
But neither it nor I
Will ever find
Life's final cause.
My grandfather is breathing into perpetuity
And cannot know where he is going,
But it is New Year's Eve,
And he will arrive somewhere
Before the night is out,
And it could be blue.

v.

We are halfway into the play.
Purpose grows,
And someone is painting
Pictures everywhere.
His palette carries every color,
And he waters his own canvas.
I know no way to avoid him.
My flesh has his hue.
He paints me without asking.
One day someone will try
To compromise me.
So we let ourselves
Come into existence
And out of it again,
Missing each other
On the threshold of
Red, yellow and blue.
There is color everywhere.
Even purple has its claim to the light.
We all have our destinies,
Each one with its own possibilities
And dangers.
Watch out for mobility and immobility:
Each one could sink you.
It is time to move,
And let the colors play just like us
Beneath the light.

vi.

Paranoia puts a stop to life.
Pain promises pain.
The needle points to zero,
Or below zero, as we dress
In our warmest clothes.
It is time to get my blood drawn.
My pain comes chilled.
That is where I will find my exercise
And practice truth upon the hill.
Love is endemic here,
And we all fall down.
Will we die first, or will love?
I cannot say,
But I know the devil
Is already out to play.
He will not come back.
He cannot eat you any more.
Our sustenance will not kill us
Any more.

vii.

The Great Father in Rome
Is looking down the wrong nose.
I think it is mine.
You cannot see his way.
He markets a monopoly
Of souls. I read them,
And see more than they can see in me.
Religion is a comfort perennially,
And I will make you uncomfortable
If you understand me.
The wind is now blowing
Away from you.
The odor is not fine.
I come from a sheltered family.
As we roll on by,
What Titan looms?
What pain comes next
To try us?
If you ask me what to do,
I will point your eyes towards your feet
And tell you to walk on.
I am looking for release.

viii.

The Decalogue

The Decalogue will shortly be complete.
It does not compete with its competitors.
It sleeps when the rest are fractious.
It does not kill, nor excuse killers.
In the spring, it is sweet,
And celebrates mimosa and the morning glory.
Its food is honey,
And it does not cheat the shadows of its intentions.
Love is its origin,
And provides the balance to its power.
It fertilizes its own seed,
And watches its offspring
Grow into its abilities.
It divides time
Into the hearts that heal
And those that don't.
It is short,
But it is art,
And is best read
Before the crowd.

ix.

There is little left within me.
I have lent it all out,
I cannot bend my nose to odors,
Nothing touches it,
And my eyes are closed
As trains go by:
They will not wake me.
The world is round
Temporarily,
And so am I,
I have evidence for it
In my head:
My skull can be read
By the paleontologists
Who know so much.
I know nothing,
And you laugh at me.
Cruelty bedevils the deceiver.
I think there is one thing
Nobody can take away from me:
And that is, I owe my soul
To no one.
Not even God.

x.

I will survive my neighbors.
My pain is greater than theirs,
So I will earn my survival.
Grace gives me my will,
And my will guides me
To a unique end.
Do not ask me what it is,
Or I will tell you:
There is only the one pain.
I will be rid of it
After everyone else
Has found his fate.
I am not afraid
Of being alone.
That is my work,
And I will find my fate in it.
The black, the blue and the red
Make up the standard of my resistance.
I am living alone with myself at last.
I have made everything else go up in flames,
And I am what is left.
When I go, there is nothing.

SPECIFIC GRAVITY

You, poem, are hanging me.
You wear black
And demand that I tell the truth
Or forfeit you.
I offer to love you, and
You wipe my face
Like a baby.
You blow my hair back behind my ears
So that I can hear your tunes.
You own me.
My ears are your supplicants,
I come bearing gifts
Like the Greeks,
But you do not acknowledge me.
You have hijacked my body.
You are the miracle inside me.
You create me.
You try to tell me who I am,
But I am afraid to hear.
You are the heat in my blood,
The creature I see
When I look inside my creativity.
I make you over and over again,
Then you make me.
I am as surely defined
By you as any line that I ever heard.

I blow out more and more poems
Just like you,
And you build my world upon your
Specific gravity.

ANOTHER END

I love you.
I love you not.
I am going to speak of this until I die.
My legs crack,
And my heart goes wild.
What lives when we fall in love?
When I say, I do,
Do I become a prisoner to you?
Is love a solitary rhyme,
Especially when it is young?
I place my tongue upon yours
And tickle,
And you respond.
And then one afternoon,
False lips serve to make
Lust bloody and love abused.
As division blooms,
We are curled alone,
And unaware
Of anything we might have known
Beyond this slip of Heaven
That consumes.

I CRY INSIDE

I cry inside.
No tears fret my face,
The amber light dies,
Verse escapes me,
The trees make shadows
In the yellow breeze,
And night arrives.
Who lives next to us?
Who are our neighbors?
Can they hear anything?
Do we know them?
Do they know us?
It would be better if we stay away from them.
Fear does not deserve an audience
In the dark.
Feelings light us up
For a while.
The mind breaks.
Time rests silently.
Some tongue promised something.
But we pass that by
Too.

THE OLD TOOTH

I am delicious.
I ply the ground
Around me with my teeth.
I eat myself
And hang a kiss
Upon your face
To dry.

I think I love myself
more now.

PSYCHOPHARMACEUTICAL

The President of the Universe
Is a silicon doll;
He tells us where to go
And how, placing his hands
On us, and spinning our heads around
Like maniacs taking
Psychopharmaceuticals
Till we drop.
I don't want my mind
To die any more.
I don't want my eyes
To run any more.
I want love massive
And perfect in action.
But that
Will not happen. I love
Like the smile on my face,
Fragrant to the rose.
I grow into myself until—
Until my live image is dead,
And I have no place
To hang my head.
Give me your well-turned thighs,
And I will come alive
To place my face between them
And taste Paradise.

ARE THERE STRAWBERRIES IN HEAVEN?

It used to be so easy:
One word, then the soup,
An alphabet of possibility.
I can cook up demons
Unasked, or bake triumphs
In crusts so that no one knows
They are there.
Even when alone, I imagine a toque
Guiding me through odors
Of fresh flesh, swimming, flying
Or dancing on the ground.

I do not return dishes.
The pewter I use is noted
For its antiquity, and the wooden spoons
Are strong enough to beat on drums.
The wire whisks fluff my hair,
And the eggs fly over me
Like missiles. I have cooked them
Until they are hard and I am brittle.
I chew my toes in anticipation
Of the great day
When I will no longer
Have to make anything.

Then I become superfluous.
I am not afraid to retire

To the sky, only
I wonder whether
Heaven offers a feast of coconut
And framboise, with ladyfingers
And dumplings, or whether
Spirits live on their own fullness,
Without food,
Adamant
As fire.

UNITED UNTIED

I'm sure
You've got a better heart than I do.
It will pack us up
In our dreams
And unify us
Like leaves licking leaves
On the ground in the fall,
Preparing to rot.

I riot.
Age arrives,
And accumulates like snow
On my head.
My hair falls out,
And my eyelids
Are competing to see
Which is dead.

Winter wraps itself around us
Like a whore before us
On her knees
Who fails to please.

Life at the end is not lovely,
And I wouldn't have gone that far alone
In search of bliss.
Only you came with me,
Then on the other side
You disappeared
And left me just the same.

A DRINK

One afternoon the future
Walked in on me
Carrying my baby time
In one hand, and in the other,
The theory of relativity.
I think I was about
To be hung in space
And then crucified, since
I had exposed
The quantum theory as hopeless.
Even God may not know everything
About himself or us.
We sit in his lap
And eat ice cream.
But we feel life poking through
And start looking for joy.
I hear my heart, it is hot,
And I realize that
I am alive.

Life could be a little long.
But I survive like the turtle in autumn:
Where do you get these things?
The critic says.
I don't know, but

The daisies speak:
The lid is on the lily,
And it listens to nobody.

THE MASKED MOVE

4:30 is the time to die.
One hand at the throat of nine,
The other flying outside time.
Perfection of the circle
Brings us to this.
We cry to ourselves
At the side of rhyme,
And watch the tears
Slide by, blossoming.
I will put your head in mine,
A secret play devised
Before a secret audience,
The fly upon the wall
Watching us fall down.
The fly will not move
Until he wants to die.
So I will not move
In your sight,
For fear you will kill me.
I do not feel myself
Move inside,
I am so terrified.
But we must place
A foot upon the floor,
And trust ourselves
To eat both sweet and sour.

We move apart,
And remain there
Once we die.
This is the choice we make
As time flies by.

LIQUEFACTION OF THE MASS

I don't think
He's aware of his pain any more,
It is so great.
Life has been lying to him
Like the devil,
And he does not cry
Or see beyond the circle
Of his eyes.
His head is swollen shut,
He has a taut brain.
The hands are limp,
The feet unshod,
And the toes numb.
Lord, could you save this child
If love would have him back?
Death does not love
And does not hate.
It only takes us away patiently
Like a warrior
Once aroused to fight
And now resigned
To move outside the light.
Someone is there, waiting
Like a shadow on the moon.
Come here, he says,
I have a home for you,
Colder than before,

But soon
You'll become
A small ball of light,
Invisible to those
With the palest eyes:
Come on, now, it is time,
It is time now, take the time
For your heavy soul to rise,
And see the world you leave
Behind you purified.

THE BALLISTIC PARTISAN

I will become ballistic
If my heart corrupts me into a fool,
Sitting away from you,
Questioning. I try the truth,
And pray that I may find you
By me, hugging
My head,
Answering me
In the dense rain.
I know you,
And the truth bends.
I play myself,
And turn myself over
To see how you feel.
I am afraid of diamonds,
The spades pick into me,
The clubs walk beyond me,
And the hearts guide me inside.
It is a long way to go,
But I saw you until today.
Now the rain falls
And I am washed out.
My years run around me,
And you stand stupefied
In front of that
Last great
Periodic
Wail.

SAY NOTHING

Nothing comes to mind.
I have studied it a thousand times,
And nothing comes to mind.
It is perilous
To look over the precipice
And see only yourself
Suspended,
Hanging by eternity,
Remembering life's warm advantages,
The heart's vagaries,
The limp of the soul
And the esteem
We bring to them.
We look down
And stand on air.
We fly around the world
Like lost angels in gray.
We finish where we began,
With nothing before and after,
Perhaps a little laughter
To lead us over
The pain of being afraid.

THE SHADOW POEM
OR
THE LITTLE GIRL AND THE BIG MAN
OR
THE BIG GIRL AND THE LITTLE MAN

Were you to catch me alive,
I would eat you alive
Like a plum, or a cinnamon
Stick boiled in rum:

I would float over you
Resonant like a tongue, sprinkled
With tea or Sweet William or
A small pinch of cardamon.

Do not accept
Wary kisses, the hiss of the snake,
Or the newts' orange scrum.
Sometimes you can fall for love

Without caution, and sometimes
Your blood will run green
As the toad's bulging eyes
Or the boiling green shore of the ocean.

PASSING

Wait, Mistah!
Who put the jewel in that crown?
Are my eyes new,
Or am I seeing things?
I have fallen into you,
And it makes no difference
What I say — the sky remains
Blue, and its temper green.
I am green, too,
And grow like grass
Cut to the root.
Dandelions proliferate
Where I am,
And the wild strawberry,
That creeps beneath my touch,
Trying to hide.
I cannot hide from you.
Love can be long.
I wear mine like a sheet
White at dawn
And ruby at noon.
In the dusk it turns purple
And blue, and then
Black at night save for
The simple pricks it gives itself.
I try to count the score
Between us, but there is none,
Only the red tally

That carries the blood
Around the head and heart
And into the same
Incontinent pain
That made me
Want to hide from you.

THE MOURNING DOVES

I will not sweat tears for you;
I will not cry into your eyes for you
And kiss them with my tongue.
I will stand aslant over you,
Placing my hands on your waist
As I rise with the horizon
To let you go below me,
Laughing at your laugh,
Hearing you for the first time.
I begin to realize what I have been.
I have been foolish:
You are a star at night,
And I can't see.

Ladies of eighty fall
In love with me
And perplex everyone.
They preen themselves
And expect more than a mirrored kiss.
I am the bent reed
In the corner,
And I cannot carry a tune.

Sometimes I think love
Can rise to blue,
Then I watch it
Disperse like mist;
We woo like mourning doves,
Driven apart by the expected kiss.

A PLAINT

Pull up your pants!
God knows what discretion
Will bring you
Outside an empty bed.
That leg is showing on your body,
And your hand is busy publicly
Being blatant.
I'll put my head
Where you want it. Now stop,
And watch out for real love.
I can feel you with these,
My eyes,
Yet you decline
Before me.
Your rose is growing cold,
And the sun melts over us
As though it had always been there,
Red.
One day, brown, we will rise
Over the sky,
Over our love,
And put our heads down low.
What can you see in a rose, cold,
Making its train invisible?

THE LOSS

The coleanthus bears reckoning.
It is sweet in the garden,
And supports the dill.
The bordering thyme
Is on its knees
Then falls to the frost in autumn.
I am lost in you like the thyme
In the other herbs.
There is no good way to say it,
Except that I would die
If you wanted.
For nothing, for your eye on mine,
Or the feel of our felicity.
You make me see infinity
In you,
So I think I can always
Be with you.
I know I have no rival
Except the breeze,
That kisses you closer
Than I can. I am afraid
That when it rains,
I will lose you
Again and again.
I am waiting for you.
My sight goes slack,
And my tears drift down
My cheeks into my mouth,

Giving me something
To drink at last.
Blood dries fast.
I think I am free,
As though you
Had never given
Anything to me.

OUR BACKYARD

We'll work on it again.
Our lines collect the blowfish as we trawl;
Young snails crawl to the fire
Under the cook's eyes,
Rolling their shells on the hot iron
Before they die.
Snails cook quickly,
Looking for the damp leaf mold
Of their native soil.
The woods move with animals
Big and small,
And men are the biggest of all, —
With their guns and shells.
I would shoot my quills at them,
If I were a porcupine,
Or turn my tail to them and run
Like a skunk.
Men have their smell,
And give themselves away
When they bathe.
The deer see with their heads in the air,
And the fashionable hunter
Has no chance
Against all the calls
The doves and the quails
Make in their own backyard.
The world's an easy place for none,
And Nature holds her hand
To every head as though she held a gun.

THE PINK PERIOD I

We will turn the tale over
To view the ink spots
And serious deletions.
The end of sense
In every line
Is a path from mind
To matter, holding the reader
Responsible for the story
Of his life
And its startling proximity
To the devilish onset
Of silence: no type,
No cast, no offer of sound
From the tongue
Or other assistance.
Who can beat the men in power
That read creed into everything,
And ask for the body,
Not love?
Even the artist
Is not equipped for self-defense,
Only self-interest
And the hope that one day
We will recognize his words
As they stand
On everyman's tongue
At the end of a long life.

The word is the gambit I make,
And I will send my soul
Into what I can't know,
If only I can try to speak of it.

THE PINK PERIOD II

To save myself
I must write myself
Out of that trial by existence
That wins no prizes,
Only a pink slip
From adversity
In the elegant atmosphere,
Where one coin
Can pay the debt claimed by all
Sooner than the saving face.
Pink is the color
Of the setting moon,
We hide under it,
A crackle in the underbrush
That only the bright can hear.
This noise is my shadow,
The touch of warning to my ear,
That contracts my other senses.
My soul is fully fleshed,
And my head riderless,
My bones are old,
My heart wavers between "yes" and "no".
Do I want love back?
Do I dare ask for sex?
Or is this only a memory
I share with myself?
I repeat the past.
I grow old,

I have been looking for that truth again,
And I can say it is the elusive peer.
I shall finally be glad to find it,
After I have already died, —
And then I at last will have shown you
Death as empty
And love apotheosized.

THE RAINBOW

A pretty variable in life
Is the length of your lashes,
That you try me by,
That keep me from you,
Like a night swallow,
Riding sparks from the fire
You have made of me.
I am wandering
Like a prophet
Through a story with no end,
Only a beginning:
If I push
I end up with nothing
Except sand,
A dry heart, no love.
You feed my feelings,
My head a casket
That is out of place
In this game.
I do not live on the sweetness of cherries
Or apricots. My tongue speaks a distant language,
And milk does not offer its sweet lips to me.
I have been sabotaged.
I am a victim of insolence
And revenge. The extreme
Report on me.
I will not protect myself,
Only, I will tell what I know

To the sky
And watch the rainbow fall
Where it is not wanted,
Unrecognized.

A LONG WALK

The heat lies low.
Now we go back
To the cedars above the graves,
Wishing the moon full,
The stars close,
Our blankets warm.
I wear fur in winter,
And cannot feel my toes
As I walk around the snow
In the empty summer garden.
The rows are still at attention,
Withered leaves visible,
Victims.
Rotten apples lie within the orchard,
Food for worms.
The cold does not comfort us.
We live on dreams
And try to remember ourselves.

I cannot believe
What I need to write poetry.
Now I am back bickering,
Demanding an idea,
My times have been so hard.
I look myself up in the dictionary
And wish I could find a guide.
Will we ever come together?

Will a poem or two
Bring you to my side?

I am writing a monument
Made of bronze,
That will last longer
Than the ages.
I think it will satisfy our eyes.

WHO THERE IS

My head is open.
My self-consciousness disarms me.
I am wandering through my history
Picking cherries and gathering apples.
Love left some time ago.
I forget when, but
I saw it go on two legs.
The sun has come over me,
And the night lies awake.
Your little love is here to comfort me,
And you guard my soul
Like the saint you are.
How did I arrive here?
Where have I been?
I have forgotten the story.
I must have been blind
Or an outcast.
Yes, I have been everywhere
I ever wanted to go.
I will end up bald in a ditch
With muddy water running
Over me.

I cannot spell any longer.
I cannot count my toes.
I am looking at my body for a sign,
But none comes.

Where is the comfort of the end?
I want to love myself again.

I am only being
What everyone else is.
I shall park myself at the door.
Can you let me in?

I don't have fire power tonight.
My tongue lisps as it swells
In my throat, and the words
That I watch come out of me
Are distant,
Like crows battered by the black wind
On their feathers.
There is no warmth there,
Only the color of disease
Infecting the trees
Arranged to take the breeze
And entice families
Of deer out to graze
In the summer dust
Until we hunt them down.
We eat meat silently,
Stripping flesh from bone
And hanging the male
Above us on the wall
To signify our animal
Superiority.

Now I am the prey,
Open to the arrow
Chance throws my way.
Let me hope, monetize my pain,
The currencies of love and hate
Are practically the same.

THE PYRE

The arabesque of violence
Does not feed on your head
As it does mine:
My property is not exclusive
Nor for sale,
I wander over its wide limits,
Shaking my fingers at myself,
Denying intransigence.
What is real here?
We do not know ourselves
Now, despite our claims.
What drove us out of power
Must have been our nature,
Disappearing.
Love once found us,
But where is it now?
In the tomb?
Or is it somewhere else
And alone?
Proud love,
Look at what you took
And what you left behind,
That was not the beginning
But the end of your road.

THE LILY ON MY HAT

Lily on my hat,
Why are you smiling at me?
Why are my ears falling down
Before you? Where is the strength
In your lips, your white body,
Your heady Priapus?
You are stately
As a masquerade, you have
Love written all over you—
What can you turn to
When you fade?

One day, no kiss
Will come to touch you,
No breath to animate you,
No spectacle to put the red
Back into your sighs.
Lily, you are dying,
You are dying
Like the nightshade,
You are dying
Right before your own
Impossible blue eyes.

MY PRACTICAL PENTAGON

i.

Make me a copy of myself
Without machines.
I am only natural.
I would like to eat my eyes,
But when they reach my stomach,
They have their reaction.
So I eat lettuce and tomato
Sandwiches, and try the
Salt and pepper in my hair.

ii.

Age is unthinkable for the neophyte,
And life is a ladle full of spices.
You do not need to hold yourself
Back. The great elephant Time
Will give you a wash
And let you go only after
You have offered him a seat at your spliced feet.

I am eating myself again,
And I think that is why volcanoes
Are erupting around me in the clouds.

EMPTY BESIDE

I will keep writing it
Until it is finished.

There is so little courage in the air.
Faith is a problem,
And fame is blind.
I take life like a pill.
Love contains the admonition
To be responsible, but who
Wears that coat?

In the winter,
Many drop out of the running.
When you ask someone for an explanation,
He hides in violence.
The wife is overcome,
Silence has infected the lambs
For the rest of their lives
And the sheep are slaughtered
Over their heads
Until all we can see are orphans.

I begin to think that
The heart is cold,
That the blood
Has been deposited
On the washroom floor,
And that there will be
No one around to clean it up.

Whose invention is this?
Am I truly a Colossus
Standing over Rhodes?
Or a triangle in a Freudian symphony?
I am prodigal,
And hang on the teeth of the night
Surreptitiously,
And perform my life
Without authenticity.

TROUBLES LEAVING

Please turn your ear
Towards mine. I have
A lifetime's griefs to give you,
To begin with: why am I here,
Playing the goat at night,
And lying in the rattling sunlight
Of the dawn?
A rostrum is not tall enough
To speak for me.
I am the guest at the empty banquet,
Afraid of the missing crowd
That will prove to me
That I was always alone.
Love once flew here,
But I shot it down.
I do not know which way
To point myself.
It is as if I were walking
Without my toes and fell
And never rose.
I practice unhappy abstinence,
And hope only
That others will have
What I lack,
And not follow where
I go.

THE WAN RIDE

I don't feel so driven
To do it as I used to.
Time is not elongating my feet any more,
And my eyes don't see
Below me.
Were I to look,
I might find the red
In my upper lip again,
Moving your love;
My lower lip
Troubles yours, and
Our mouths open
In the game we play
Before sleep.
Love is its own standard.
It moves outward
From behind the veil
We draw over it.
It is a secret
That everyone knows.
The lily sees it
In the sun.
The quaking aspen
Feels it in its leaves.
We fashion ironwood
Into instruments
That attack it like steel.
How is it in imagination so real?

I do not know,
But I play with you,
And I feel myself still.

POLARIZATION

What are we going to write
With our toes?
The acid rises to my throat
And makes me mute.
I swallow myself,
And wonder if the seed
Can lead to the end
Of my human frailty.
Silently I watch the pools
We swim in like eyes
That foam on the surface
Of our lives.
I grasp your finger-tips
And feel your hair glow:
You are a day angel,
And a sprite at night,
When the moon has much
To say to us.
We play at dice,
And love to skate
On life's thin ice
As though it were
Impermeable.
I think the morning shines
Like a fool that carried the same torch
Yesterday.
Your love lacks weight.
You eat your heart

To give your self substance.
You burn me at the poles,
But I escape,
Knowing that
Should we exchange roles,
I would hurt you first
And die first just the same.

IN THE CHAMBERS OF THE DARK

You are dead
And we are dead
And I am long
About the head:
There is no red
Like blood that's bled
Tell me what's to love
Instead

LIPITOR

You don't want to
Impress yourself too much.
You don't want
Too big a reputation alone.

Or someone
Will eat you
For breakfast
Like a grapefruit,
And with all those pills
Inside him
He may die.

I AM THINKING

I am thinking.
I know it is difficult,
But I am thinking, —
And thought is no quick boon.

Look at what it has done to me.

Your heart captures me.
Your head rolls up to my face,
And your ears slide on either side of me,
As they try to hide you behind me.

Such is the music
We have arranged:
My hair stands straight up on my head
And sings.

My teeth eat themselves in tune.

The stain is enormous,
And the sound indestructible.

And you bleed, too.

HIGH TEA

Three eyes will conquer much.
One in mind,
Two at rest,
And three at last
In Paradise.
What do you say to that, love?

PARADISE

Elaborate gains
Around Time's waist
Foretell disaster.
Let ivory and alabaster
Wear us out.
The soul inside will ambulate
Around the eyes
As though surrounded by Paradise.

HANGING ON THE RUINS OF MY NOSE

You're building on the ruins
Of my red-neck nose,
Running around so cock-sure.

The snake in the garden
is green and sleepy
in the sun,

Hiding a secret
That deceives just one.

HOT

Is there something wrong with love?
Does it stand
Or does it sit?
Illuminate or darken?

How do we find it,
A-lack-a-day away?
Why do we fight it?
I would try to like it.

I think it is hot,
Very hot,
Very hot…

KISSING A KISS

A gift indeed is
A gift needing
A recipient.
I receive you
Like a gift
With a kiss—
And kissing you
Is definitely like
Kissing true.

LEFT IN THE ORDER OF THINGS

Dear Lady,
Where have you gone?
Why have you left us
Alone in the night,
Like a child, Mother,
Waiting for dawn?
We still hear your heart beating
Somewhere in that cold body
And it keeps us warm.
Mother,
You have left us now appealing to love,
And—appealing to you—we will not come to harm.

LOOKING BACK

Hello, woe.
Are you alive,
Or am I?
I think we are dead
Together, and cross
The lawn outside
On our cracked feet.
Don't ask me what I know.
It is impossible to show
You what you do not see.
You are the lavender traveler,
And I avoid you,
Lost in propinquity.

FOLLOW ME

Ply me with extinction,
O, my heart.

I am willing to let myself go.

Now I know how to die
Out of love for you.

SIGNATURE

Love is a sign
That we live by,
That we are alive.

Who made me?
Who makes me now?
Love?

I will never know
Whom to thank.

HONEY-SUCKLE

There is more than one way
To arrive at night.
Turn the faucet on,
And it will pour out pink roses,
Posies, and other delights.
Seat yourself under the running water,
And you will smell the scent
Of honey-suckle the hue
Of delicate yellow amber.

FIN DE PARTI

Where does all that strength go,
Lingering in what remains
Of our disintegrating love?

I MUST UNDERSTAND

I must understand before I fail.
I must abolish
All my love and all the mishaps
Normal rising brings,
The legitimate offspring
Of your incredulity.

WILL YOU SINK WITH ME?

Will you sink with me
Into modern matter
Where we will find ourselves
Delivered into the shadowy
Half-life of an unborn star:
A nova not yet exploded
Yet tamed by its own weight
To stay intact until
Finally subsiding
Into a black hole,
A small universe all its own?

DISAVOWING THE MEAN

Blue at last!
I say, blue at last!

Stretching out to the horizon of grace,
Pouring flowers out of guns disarmed by tunes,—

I am not going to sleep tonight.

The Equinox is behind us,
Wearing pink and blue,
And falters—

Falters in the pursuit of truth.

MAYBE I CAN SQUEEZE

Maybe I can squeeze
One of us out of two.

Our sighs leave us alone,

And the news is bad.

Very bad.

Rain as Art

: 2000, 2005 :

RAIN AS ART

When it rains
It rains on us,

The rain is indiscriminate,
Like its cousin, dust,

The same can be said
Of a break in the heart,

For some, love may fail no matter what,

To them, love has become an art,
Art as pain, or pain as art;

When forced to take the two
As one, art and pain,

I try to think back to the rain,
I stand between these lines upright,

And faithfully look into the coming night.

OPERATOR

Operator, call 911,
Or I'll call the cops.
Operator, I'm blind,
I'm in the hospital,
I don't have a dime.
Operator, I want to talk
To an operator with brains!
Operator, it'll rain,
It'll rain on your remains.
Operator, don't hang up,
Operator, operator,
Operator, operator—
Let me talk.
Operator, I'm alone,
I'm afraid.
Operator, I'm afraid
I can't get laid.
Operator, you have a family,
I'm on my own,
My daughter hates me,
My son-in-law he's
Selling my home.
It's money they want, operator,
And the money is mine—
Operator, that's why
I don't have a dime.
Operator, you damn bitch,
You've hung up.

I've hung up myself
A thousand times, operator;
I'm an operator myself,
And I'm deaf and blind.
You'd never know it, operator,
Unless you listened to me
Long enough,
Operator, listen, listen,
I'm unique, I'm kind,
I lost myself somewhere long ago,
Operator; I'm an operator, too,
Or was, but now I don't know.
Operator, can we talk, can you be
Here with me indefinitely?
Operator, operator, don't be mean,
Operator, operator, operator,
Operator, operator, drop dead!
Drop dead like me!

IF I START IN ON YOU

If I start in on you,
If I shoot you
With my brain,
If I tell you
What I am hearing
When I watch
You moving your face in front of me,
You will believe nothing.
So I walk into the dining room
And sit down at an empty table
And eat air for breakfast.
You live on inconsequentialities
And hope that one day
I will see
That blue is the color of your hair,
That your eyes are white
With purple rims,
That you wear glasses,
Et cetera.
All this
Has gotten us
Nowhere.
What if I show
You all the insides
Of my brain,
And then turn
To you
And shoot you

With my pain?
You are standing on your soul
With strange disdain.

A LITTLE CLIP

This little man
Fell off the deep edge
Of his psyche.
And what became of him?
He grows a lemon,
A farmer in summer,
Squash in the back
Of his mother's blue sedan,
Rotting as fast as the odors
Will permit.
Play that we perform,
Someone aged will clip you.
The puck will slide fast
Over your head
And leave you tonsillated
For life, a powerful
Figure downtown.

A MAN WITHOUT A TONGUE

I might lose it,
And then where would I be?
A leaf without a tree,
A stone without durability,
A tear without an eye,
Marrow and no bone,
I would be a wanderer
Without a home.

O, Heavens, save me from my destiny,
I have not chosen it,
It has chosen me,
Or so I think,
And, yet, when the earth's
Revolutions are done,
What we are is what each one of us
Has chosen to become.

Siren, will you sing to me one to one?

PAPA

Papa, you are what I seem:

My comic feast,
My intellect,
My mind's glove,
My soul's design.

Please, Papa,
Let me down slowly,
Let me grow peacefully
Out of your arms.

WELL

When I arrived at twenty-two,
Aleph turned my head towards you,
My eyes began to roll by me,
And see your invisibility:

I learned to strike a poet's pose,
I became a Guardian of the Rose,
And in the year or two since then
I realized I'd last until the end.

The end of what I do not know,
And I do not want to know,
It is enough to have seen the sun
May's breath and autumn's purple show;

There is only one thing left to see:
I love you, do you love me?

PATIENT DAYS

Sometimes I feel a force in me,
Though only fleetingly,
It is like an athlete's zone,
Or poet's moment
Of inspiration.
What brings me there
I do not know,
Though I do know
It is very rare,
Like the wry-bill,
Or the spotted hare;
So I do not go alone
Looking for a kiss,
It must find me first,
Like love, like bliss.

NONNULLA

Death has a decided
Atmosphere: tranquil
Non-occupancy.

No one can take your death
Away from you.
It is your property.

THE PHOENIX AND THE DOVE

In Brooklyn there are no owls.
Only streetlights and taxis
And evening strollers,
Talking of business, I suppose,
    Never of the rose
    Or the absent sun,
    Or the Phoenix
    And the Dove,
    And the color
    Of their love:
    Rare birds
    Who make me feel
    That at night
    The world is real,
    That I hear
    Beneath the eaves
    The sound of swallows
    That still grieve
    Over Cadmus
    Prince of Thebes.
If you are in love, beware,
Rue can blossom anywhere,
One day we'll have it right
And learn to trust the beauty of the
    night.

MANDARIN

I will live a mandarin.
Hey, man, you very clean?
Time is short, my hair grows thin;
Hey, man, where you been?
I've been beyond the sky, you see;
Hey, man, you try to rule?
Beyond the sky you can't see me;
Hey, man, you be a fool?
I want to tell you how I feel:
Hey, man, are you for real?
As real as you, but not for sale.
Hey, man, I love you, too.
And that's the end of all I know.

POETRY

I feel like writing another one,
I am so profligate.
Words escape me,
My brain purrs,
My toes tintillate,
My stomach boils.
My groin wraps itself into knots. –
Oh poetry, you female devil,
You do this to me whenever
I think of you – merely –
And when I write,
I die.

PRUNELLA

Allowed to grow,
she would throw
her skin
like a snake in
the garden,
a thin
translucent lace
made of chased
silver.
Such a cover
would keep her
warmer
than aether or
the vapor
the sun
leaves in his run
by the one
million
Inhabitants of this world.

—for Dashiell, April 22, 2002

ODE TO TIME
OR
IS THIS THE LAND OF COMPLETE BEING?

Time: a multiple blow,
And slow.
We make mouths;
It frees us up for hope. You! Keep
A foot on the ground!
Cinnamon cannot taste like you,
Nor nutmeat nor passion-fruit.
More likely an orange.
We are all beginning to find it out:
We are being squeezed.
Time? You dirty dog!
We have been throwing you
Away.
I don't care to talk to you
Today.
You are not fair.
In fact, I am not sure
That you exist at all.
I must consult a higher Authority.
Time! You are a fraud!

ON THE ROAD

It was difficult,
The muffled dragon,
The brain hypothecated,
The Prince of Wales
In abeyance.
Do you know where
We get these things?
They make me tired,
Complaining.
My children make me tired,
I read their faces carefully
And I —
I am at the horizon
Of new possibilities:
A yam for a new potato,
Diet pepsi,
Bubble gum.

It's all for the children,
They have their horizons,
Unless we knock them down,
Which we sometimes do.
But who can knock over
The sunrise? Even the
Rain cannot keep all
The light from coming through.
The least a day can be
Is gray.

People can be gray anytime.
And children. Then they
Need more horizons,
More sunrises, a greater dawn.

SEX PAIN

I like the way you move your body,
It makes me laugh.

I dream of you
With my eyes open.

I see you by daylight
All over my field of vision.

I dress you in my imagination.
Then I undress you.

It takes guts to surrender to lust.
But I can do it.

CHRYSANTHEMUM

Chrysanthemum, why are you blue?
Or are you purple?
Or lavender, or green?
Colors change upon your leaves,
The sun's rays blow across your face,
Your petals are the eyes and ears
That hear the murmur of my fears,
I am afraid of green and red and blue:
Chrysanthemum, I am afraid of you.

THE VORTICES

Red or blue:
It's you who must choose
Between truth or beauty,
And though it's true
Truth is beautiful,
Beauty is not
Always true.

A DECLINING STAR

There is really only one evening star.
And one morning star.
They measure us.

I am in hiding.
There is nothing left for me
Between dawns.

At other times, the pain is excruciating.
I seem to fall between
Two legs.

O Lord, save me from all stars.

NO TIME LEFT

A heart is what you have
When you see someone die.
It does not buy you time,
Only understanding.
There are some who do not understand.
For them, life ends with death,
Because there is no time left.

THE WOUNDS OF TIME

The wounds of time I could not save,
Purple scar, purple heart,
Able sailor in the dark,
Save the figure on the wall,
The light that's gone,
The dark that's art.

I cannot read myself alone,
The crimson lupine's gone astray,
The marigold will have its way,
The common vetch will never say
What it is I cannot know
About the quiet dawn that's come,

I can hear the bluebells tingle,
And the lily blow its drum.

DEBTS

If you saved the world,
Who would thank you?
Who would be left
To say, "Yes,
It is a fine day
At last and we are joyful."
The timpani will play
Into the evening,
And the people will remove
To the parlors
Of the great palaces,
Out of the sun at last.
Tongues will move
In novel ways,
Swinging from tooth to tooth
Without losing their feeling.
Alive can be good,
It is time to shrink our debts;
Move over, true love is gaining in value.

ROW

Let's see.
Ambergris colors the morning
In the window.
The night sky is white
With stars revolving around the poles,
Cancer catches its tail,
Pegasus laughs out loud
At the twins caught in
Non-idiosyncratic sin,
Andromache nurses her heart
As she tries to keep
Her rivals apart.
Odysseus, where is your veil?
How can you see so much
And still survive?
Where is your tongue, your
Golden throat, your speaking heart?
You are the veteran
Traveling home wave by ponderous wave,
Sailing through the Mediterranean maze.
Take your oar, great man,
You are telling us what you know,
Life moves in circles
However straight we row.

PROCEED, WISH

Wonder, put it in your hat,
A flower like a daffodil,
And a rose for the unborn,
No one sees the sun with scorn,
What we know is what we have,
Some do love to no avail,
But life is not an empty glass,
Save us from ourselves at last,
God, we love you,
Let us pass.

AT THE AGE OF FIVE

In memory of Sam

There is a wild man in my mind.
I can see him going blind:
He's a friend of the poor, like you and I,
But he's going blind, and he can't see why.

Oh, man, poor man,
You sit on your perch, your little stool,
And I begin to think that life is cruel,
That life is cruel and we are fools.
I think my blind friend is going to die,
And there is no way to save him—
Whether I speak the truth to him or lie.

This young patient of God is five,
There's only one day more
He'll be alive.
By God's grace I don't see why.

PEPSICO PIPELINES, COCA-COLA CONDUITS

It turns your life upside down
and leaves you to dry out
or die on your own

So you wander around on
a cloud and write letters
you can't mail

and look for sex in
some place new for you
where you won't find any

And then you go back
to Coke because the demon
keeps you company when

you're cold as an ice-cake
and you think life
has always been like this

and for you it has, because
your memory's shot: Pepsico
shot it down a long time ago

WHAT WILL HAPPEN?

It is time:
Transferring laps
From leg to leg,
Running behind the clock.
The lines are all drawn up
On our faces,
And we are laughing
At the corners
Of our eyes.
We are running away with the clock, and the sun is ticking overhead
Like a bomb.
I think it is thermonuclear
And very warm.
Can you tell me when it will stop
Or when the Universe will end?
I can. When we say, "Pop".
Three letters and some breath
Altogether
And it will end.
And can you tell me
What will happen then?

BRUEGELLANDE

Bruegellande, grotesque and ribald,
rallies round the medieval moralists.

Raised forecastle and quarterdeck,
grim black Napoleonic Jack
on the mast,
the first mate a ruin,
the admiral a skeleton,
the captain an acrobat.
On his knees he holds
a woman covered with sores,
no nose
naked under a shroud, combative, savage and frolicsome.

Next comes the battle of the shrouds:
devils' masks, pigs' snouts,
muzzles, tusks and asses' ears,
a menagerie clucking, bellowing
and whistling
like a grackle on the poop:
le diable qui pêcha merveilles

A titular see
le soleil se couche
febrile decay and sterility
    dogs howl

CHANTICLEER

I try to see
The earth as blue,
It's hard to trust
Another hue
From above
The atmosphere,
Where the view
Is icy clear.
The earth as blue
Is like a tear
On the face
Of Chanticleer,
From down below
It must appear
That love is gone,
But he's still here:
Poor Chanticleer.

A SHADY TERMINUS

A short, harsh cry to say hello:
I cannot smile plainly,
Upcoming events overwhelm me,
The news is a terrible joke.
I have no love-impulse, no desire,
I live on ice,
I'm tired.
Lies keep me alive.
I am afraid —
The light beyond me
Is the light beyond the grave.
I play only in my sleep.
My dreams deceive.
Can you smell out my pain?
The rot?
The fear?
The soil?
You play to gain.
I even like you.
I have passed my life
In your shade.
Now I cannot play.
I breathe a bit.
I have air to live on.
I am elementary again.
I am one by one.

FORTY

Forty was my goal,
Now that I am forty-five,
I am not sure
As spring appears, that
I should be alive.
Daffodils, tulips and crocuses
Have not pleased me
Since I was young.
Now they begin
To bring me back
To their patient show
Of love.
Forty was my goal,
Now that I am forty-five,
I am more sure
Than I ever was
That I should be alive.

WHERE DID HE GO?

We'll all be gone by suppertime,
If we insist
On being prime:
Head at games
And heart at mind,
We try to leave
Our peers behind:
There must be room
For all of us,
In the shade
Or by the sun,
If not, then
Everyone's undone.

—In memory of Yeats

PERIOD OF TREASURE

Align your self with me,
Turn your cockles a bit awry,
As though eating shellfish;
Publish your thoughts
In the latest Bulletin,
Which everyone can misunderstand,
Pretend you're a clam
And cannot talk,
Living beneath the sand;
Someone will have faith in you,
Someone, only one, will die for you,
And you will never know who or why they do,
And in the end,
When you are forced to cry above the trees,
Your tears will speak
Greater volumes than the seas,
And one day you will find
The one who loved you most
Set you free.

THE QUESTION

Let us demonstrate how I do it:

I poach my eyes,
I boil my nose
I fry my hair,
I dice my ears,

I make a dish
Of my own fell,

Then I know
What I can sell:

Avoid the world,
The world is Hell.

THEY

They have to accept me as I am,
I call myself outrageous,
Telling the truth in dandified
Smiles. We laugh; we don't
See where threats got us.
Life is funny when you least expect it.
We expect pain from a pinprick.
But there is nothing there:
Only the light and the blue moon
And the dandified air.

TIME AGAIN

I am a map full of particles.
You are what I know.
Will you clean me?
Will you love my dirt?
Will you put your nose
Between my legs?
You tickle me
And it hurts.
You're nuts to me, deathtrap.
I cannot take you out anymore.
You embarrass me.
Your sky is worn out,
Your moon eclipsed,
Your sun a shell.
There is a little blue
Left from my sky,
But not enough
To seduce anybody.
You have been scrutinized.
We can no longer use the truth.
Someone has just told us
We are missing.

ENEMY

Are you my memory?
Do you touch my neck
With your teeth
And threaten to sink them into
Me? I cannot tell
What you think about me,
You are so far away
When you stand next to me.
It is as though my heart
Had collapsed, and the rest
Of my body were hiding
The truth. Tell me, O sage one,
Where am I to lie?
How can I cry?
What do you care to make me do?
I fear,
I fear,
I fear
I shall end up
Loving you.

TRY TEA

Try tea.

Let us loose upon the cloth,
To imitate the evening moth
That dines
Upon the moon:
You cannot hide it
From the eyes
Of everyone that turns himself
Upon its shape.

Daggers to hearts do tend,
Moth, fly fast, my only friend,
I wish us both a speedy end.

L'AVENIR

I can write anything at any time of day;
There is no way you can stop me:
My mind will write,
My pen will speak,
My tongue will move volumes
Through the atmosphere—
And you will have to hear
It all, whether you want to or not.
Because you will have chosen to
Open your ears,
And they will take me in—
All of me—
And all your sin
And all our history,
Until we die,
And even then
There will be others
Left to hear
What is left
Of enmity and fear.

EPITHALAMIUM

Who died in April?
I think it was I.
April, I think, was very cruel,
As time went by,
And I was made to die for love,
And I was made to die.

       — for all those who have died of AIDS

Youth and Age

: 2012 :

YOUTH AND AGE

We have to wait until ten o'clock.
That is when the bees sleep,
Our mind begins to wane,
And the night-time honey
Is available.
Turn over on your back,
And I will show you
How sweet you are—and salty—
And how I eat you
Like something delicate
For dessert, the day's work
Having provided the main course
For my appetite.
Turn again, and we can kiss
Until dawn and approach the light.
We live by our eyes
As in a dream, daring
To love. You are young,
And I have seen too much
To pursue you beyond the least obstacle.
My skin is stained
By age. A page forward
For me only reminds me how
Little text to life is left.
I have death to face,
And you have only love.
Love and death lie everywhere
As in a sea:

Both wear me down.
In you I can escape
Until I drown.

THE ULTIMATUM

I can't help it:
I might try perdition.
It is so convenient
To cut off
Your own head.
It leaves you
Like Saint Denis,
Basking in the sun,
Holding your crown
In front of everyone,
No longer any mouth
Or brain to feed,
All that a poet can summon
As ultimatum.

LISTENING

When, first, Liz died,
Then my father,
I waited for a signal
From God, the touch
Of a wing in my ear.
And there was no sound,
Only my body watching theirs;
And we became the silence
Around us; and I wanted a stratagem
To stir my quick breath,
And give me back my ear,
So I could listen to their death
And take back what life
Had hidden there.

ROUNDING OUT

If the world were not round,
The sound
Of its rotation
Would be shrill,
Like a dying engine
Turning against its will.
Turn yourself, love,
Into my arms;
All the alarms are done
And the races won or lost—
You can have me now
Without hiding.
I have died
A thousand times
And two thousand more
Waiting for you—
One more time
And I shall love you
A bit less than before,
Only for eternity,
So much says death to me,
And I believe him.

A SALLOW SEASON

Maybe I can work in the morning,
The work is drab
And the season sallow.
I like this time of day
That brightens me,
Very gray,
Like the ash
That keeps me
On the path
Heavenward.

THE BEE DYING

There is a step awry
In the movement
Of the eye,
He cannot see
The honey, his
Own baggage,
Or his death nearby,
Though he smells it,
And realizes
He will die poisoned
Far away from his hive
And his lost
Dance of discovery.

Love is his right,
Self-sacrifice his fate
In the nectar he takes.
There is no sword
Small enough
To seize him—
Only the poison
That undoes him.

He waves his friends away.
His time is small,
But his presence in it
Is beneficial
Almost to all.

ETWAS, ZUM BEISPIEL

For Uncle Herb on his ninety-fourth birthday

You've got things ordered at the last.
But the present presents a chance
To last a while beyond
The usual end.
We know no one like you,
Musician or acrobat or friend,
Bringing fire to light the night.
You dance with the choir
Of your mind,
Hung with the graces of age,
Keeping the long days at bay,
Outlasting the spring snow
That melts over the wet fields
You have already sown.
They have grown with you,
And you have lived happily
Through the summer and fall.
In winter you reach for
The warm age inside you.
One day you will try the dark,
And willingly find a new way
To secure your heart.
What role you play next,
What stage and what text,
Is the secret of another time
That lies ahead,

Not decked with fear,
But with patience
And tenderness.

LOVE IS LIKE…

Love is like an instrument
In an orchestra,
And sometimes like the orchestra itself,
When in bliss,
Rather than the sole note
That carries through the night alone,
Rather than the light of day
Which shows its face
With every tone.

FREE FOR FAME
OR
FAME FOR FREE

We cannot remember
When we were unknown,
Yet the general dissatisfaction grew
Deep in the seed of those
Who knew you.
We remain what we were,
And the shadows weep for obscurity
And the tongues lash themselves
To the roof of ours mouths,
And give pain
To anyone who tries to set them free
And find the truth of love.
I have no tongue.
No one revolves around me.
The lawyers still sell their wares
To the unwary,
And the poets pronounce
On inconsequentialities,
And the politicians
Seek power.
Some look for permanent fame.
No one is permanent—
Even a king wears thin
Beneath the rain and ice.
We read the Bard,

But he never
Reads the same twice.
And were he to return to earth,
He would find his work
Alien, singing an unfamiliar tune.
Who writes, writes for himself
And two or three.
One day I will turn upon you
And your tongue
And set both free.

SOME DAY I WILL STOP

Some day I will stop,
And that is the day
I will die.
My moving trial
Turns aside the judge
Called Time,
A small cushion for my father's cheek
Of bone that accompanies
All openings,
Works are central
To the main body
Of the life,
A joy that is free
To the dark-skinned and
The light alike.
I don't want to counter-balance
Your weight with mine.

My tongue turns bright blue,
Its new and native shade.

Where is the rumor
That started all this anyway?
Is love living off itself?
Does death
Defy everything?

I push you out the door,
And all you do
Is vomit on the floor
And copulate with my enemies.

The rain brings us back to reality.
It is night-time,
And the low watch will be over soon,
Before we win our case
Or lose.

FACES

Through silence
I cannot be manipulated.
The hand grows weak
That tries to plant itself
In me; my neck is fully occupied
Holding the fort;
The chest encloses heat,
The lungs oxygenate,
And my member
Stands prepared to take advantage
Of advantage
Whenever it occurs.
I admit it:
My feet are due for replacement,
New soles and toes,
And nails to hold them in place.
I watch out for the fungal
Variety of rot in every
Corner of the commonplace.
Who will taunt me?
And who will advertise my grace?
I am no neophyte,
Only quiet in abstinence.
There is no way
For anyone to get where I am.
I have been arriving for a long time,
And I pass my destination
As though I had forgotten
To disembark the train.

I think I am going
To live forever,
And if I don't,
My fall will go unnoticed,
And my death will be crowned
Without a face.

BIG BIRTH

I wear life like a cup of tea,
So liquid and diffuse,
Or a gold staff diversified
By ivory and ebony.
My breath is not so precious
As your love,
Nor your heart so deep
As this reminder
That will not corrode with time.
My mind is big,
My time is big,
You fill up my body
With pleasure and fantasy,
And now that I am fifty-one
I wonder what God and man
Will make of me.
I court sedentary
Revolution,
And live for the lilac
And the crocus in the spring,
Both purple and white.
I was once alive,
And I am losing ground
To an age I created
Out of hand.
As I wait to die,
I see the world is not so big
As it used to be,
And neither
Are you or I.

PEONIES

Were they all right, the shadows?
Can I live in them?
Do they live in me?
Is their first instance their last,
Or is fate itself always shadowy?
My love is tired sometimes.
And I wonder at my luck sometimes
In not following,
In not accepting the rain
That brings me down to the edge
Of the sea,
Impatient for pleasure.
The tulips propagate
In the front garden,
And the side of the hill
Is full of daffodils
In spring, when everything
Seems to be rising,
Flying up to meet us
As we walk through the new grass
Touching space.
Spring proceeds,
And its flowers fall into the neat earth,
Where June blooms:
The tiger-lily
And the rose and the purple peonies.
They show me a way to set them free
When they kiss their roots

At season's end.
Then they pass with a smiling sigh,
For they know that they will always come again.

APOSTROPHE

Shed your principles
And you sell some tears.
The back of harmony
Breaks, too, when sympathy
Falls slack at the touch of cold.
I am afraid,
I am afraid you
Will chafe me,
Or your silence
Choke me,
Or make my brain ache,
That I will have to face
You alone,
And find nothing there.
Eat the flowers,
Pour wine on my hair,
Walk with me again
As though we depend
Upon a single thread. I see
Your shadow in the dark, you were
Once a king of art,
And now you sound
A simple tone:
An old bundle
Of blood and bones.

THE VOICE OF SILENCE

There are three tribulations to discover.
Can I live up to them?
Or is my soul too sensitive,
Too sensitive to know them?
One is love, one pain,
In all their perfections,
And one the shady light
That lightens the darkness
Of the night. I wish
I could feel you there,
But the swallow is gone
With the fall, and the daisy
Left a long time ago. I cannot
Count you any more, you are
So small in me—I cannot
See you inside anymore,
I have doubled the lock
That shut you out
And kept me in. I count love's
Tired hour, now swept
Like leaves
Or the dust that seizes
Our traces in the summer. The eye
Of dawn will not blink
At us rising any more,
And the muscle that we
Expected to feel is flaccid.

Tie your horns tight,
Wastrel—I love you still,
And try to lie to keep you here,
And, loving, fail.

LOOK, MOTHER

Look, Mother,
I am your brother,
I unwind by you,
Invisible.
I am not happy
In the caste
You have given me.
I am an unwilling baby—
A stranger at my own front door.

I grew inside you,
And appeared in the casual light
Of a June morning,
Blind and small,
At the start frightened of the cold
Clothes you wrapped around me.
I saw your eyes above me
As I looked for your breast,
Which at first I didn't find.
You poured your milk
Through my teeth,
And swallowed my breath.

I was King here
For a day.
Then I turned away from infancy,
And let my older sibling
Trouble me

For a while.
But even that pain
Resolves itself—
I was bright enough to see
That I could drown my brother
With a smile,
And my brother could never
Drown me.

HOURS OF AN AGE

They are all done.
Deposit windows on their heads
So they can see, then
They are defrauded of their innocence,
A cabalistic taboo
Hanging over them
Like the one that undid
The prophet they could not leave alone.
A time will come
For them again,
When the spring blooms,
And certainty is keen
To assert itself,
When love turns,
By turns coarse and smooth,
Bearing shared dragons,
Nimble on their feet
And in no need of targets
For their tongues.
They were all once babies,
And it shows in some.
Tulips were once green,
And the leaves of the heliotrope blown
As well as the blossom.
Spice was once a leaf alive
And young, and so was
The rest of possibility.
Purpose is in creativity.
Let it be: it will be restored

To itself when we
Fail to count hours,
And tongues twist by empty teeth
At the sound of final, shared travail.

THE DEAD DOG

It is so strange, Creation.
What was He thinking of
When He painted my face?
Where did the dog go
That He unleashed?
Life has become dangerous
Around the back door
And by the alley
Where the sugar-plum ladies
Used to dance.
Do you call me something there?
I am innocent and cannot
Use my tongue.
I am a policeman not allowed to go anywhere
Or see anyone.
The path to the back
Has been closed to me
For a long time.
When I open the gate,
I am beginning to win,
But I have not yet won.
The rose in front is for the ladies.
I am not a ladies' man.
I do not like strawberry-blondes,
I do not eat creme-covered sugar-plums,
And I do not get fat.
I dive through the gathering night
Like a bat.

I can see you.
I feel you down below,
But I am not allowed
To fall in love with you, no,
So I have an occasional fling
With practically anything,
And throw my life
Into an empty ring,
Into a place where I find nothing—
Only the yellow corpse of a dog that died
Yesterday looking for water.
He should have found it,
Only it was underneath his chin,
And his huge nose had stopped functioning.
Had he known,
Had he noticed me,
He could have drunk
From my eyes
And cried
All the way home,
Alive.

I RIGHTLY FLY

This is what I do
For a living.
What do you suggest?
Ice cream? Le gigondas?
Are the waters willing
To take a bathe
In their own calm?
Or are they flowing
To Antarctica
To end up
Frozen in my mind?
I have been behind
The wheel all day,
And sleep pushes me forward.
The slots that are my eyes
Go into overdrive,
And the sun
Fails to illuminate the way.
How do you surprise
A dead duck?
Where does history begin?
Where does it end?
Where does the worm's soul go
When the worm is dry?
Do sparrows die intestate?
Is there a will
That can direct me
To my end?

Or shall I stay rolled up
In your history,
Until something really develops?
I don't care.
Your body is before me,
And I am lying down ready to
Receive it free.
Don't make me pay,
Or I shall fall down
And never rise beside
Your eyes again.
You cry,
And I am uncontrollable
Until I see the future
Dimly outside.
There is really
Nothing there,
But I love you anyway,
And wonder how
We got there that way.

PAINTING LATE

It's too late.
The night is turning twelve,
At one the bats bite
The dark, and the stars
Guide mariners across
The freezing seas
That winter gives the hemisphere,
Like a house of ice,
Lying across roads
That lead into trees
Hidden by snow.
I go behind you,
Trying to make out
Your limbs in the white haze:
The pink of your cap
And your red nose
And black boots,
And the wide scarf
That hangs around your neck
Keeping you warm
For my warm lips.
I kiss you,
And the snow dissolves,
And your frozen eyelids
Slide open again
And see me
Above you, wide open
Below the sky

As though we were
Children.
My eyes are blue
And they treat you
Like a surprise
That will only take place
Sporadically,—
Before the sky floats up
And leaves us
Both standing alone,
Separated by a tune:
Self-love loves alone,
And so I do,
I end up loving no one,
And cannot plant upon your lips
A kiss now overdue.

THE CRITIC

What's inside the head?
Emolument?
Traces of aphrodisiac?
Or love's painted horns?
There is an ambush here,
Waiting for the innocent
With twenty
Or twenty-five years
On his head.
I would give him seven
Chances out of ten to
Die and go to
Heaven,
Where he will be
Received as a new-born youth:
His soul is clean,
And his heart lacks the mass
That age brings—
These are not things poets
Treat lightly.

I turn my back
To fly up with you.
The dove circles,
And we move beyond
The earth's blue eye;
We shall die only
Once for lack of fame—

Your verse is composed
Of ink-stained lace
Beyond the touch
Of our opponents' minds.
They move like deer,
And are afraid of ambush
From behind.

SPARROW FLEEING

I bought a lot of food.
I bought a lot of you, too,
Edible and inedible.
Indelible. My mind now flies
Past you, delicacy.
My tongue ignores
Yours, wavering between
Your teeth like
A wanton flag.
I cannot be gunned down
Any more.
I cannot hear your tears fall down
Any more.
Your teeth no longer smile
At me, and your lips
Have turned pink with envy.
I love myself at last
As I find myself
Abandoned. I have
Adopted myself
Like a quiet child.
You remain unruly
Beneath me, but I
Am saving you.
The elms are whistling,
The pomegranate flourishes
In the dark,
And the sparrow falls

Off the mark.
In that sparrow, I see you.
Put yourself where I stand:
My head scrapes the ceiling
Of the sky,
Time will eventually slay me,
Shocking no one, except, perhaps,
You and I.

WORK

Poems fill in the breach
Of affection,
Turning a lack
Of introspection
Into the currency
Of false love.
Turn outside in,
And you will feel
Untempered heat,
Lust, jealousy
And a greedy heart.
Allow yourself more
Temperate latitude,
And you may find
Your love comes more willingly
To you.

EXIT AT BIRTH

For Roger Shattuck

You can choose the day
Of your death,
Or you can wait for it.
God is impartial and patient
With the penitent
And non-penitent alike.
We comprise one body,
An upright sign
In the mind
That something is going
Left or right—
Sinners trying to move back
Through the steps of time
Behind them where they cannot see
But only indulge in retrospect,
And there is no advantage in that.
Propose progress
And know nothing about where you go
Except that snails move faster and know less.
And when their eyelids droop
It is a fascinating calamity for them.

What is the purpose of this music? you ask.
It is universally the same
In summer or winter.
I am putting my head

Under the water,
I am breathing through
My neck like a fish,
As my gills crack
And my head slopes up.

And that's where I'll be
When you come
And try to change places
And find I am unwilling,
That you can't just
Have life your way
Without loving me.

THE DROWNED TURK

Come, and I should play.
My head is just a mess.
Pliny has told his history on me,
And I offer myself to him
Like a Christmas present.
We celebrate the New Year
As though it were here,
But it has yet to unfold
In front of us,
And if we turn away from it too soon,
It will fall down
And roll to a further room.

The phlox loves used loam,
And other leaves
Blow across the balconies
Of the lifeless.

Life is a huge mausoleum
We live in but don't see;
This state is not temporary.

The fox trot
And the waltz
And the polka
And the samba
Will teach you how to hold your nose
Up where it can't be seen or used

While you wait.
Your tide is floundering.
You are not able to swim,
Nose alone,
But you can taste the water
In your salt
Until your blood tells you
Something is wrong
With your circulation.

I suppose the moment is paramount,
But if you leave your body behind,
You may recognize
What the Deity had in mind
When you were born:
I think He forgot to tell you,
"These are my arms."
You slid right into them
Like a ripe plum.

A MEDITATION

I have to paint
A picture of my soul,
Red, green or yellow,
The bees know,
And fritillaries blow
Through the breeze
That flows around them.
Nature never sleeps.
There is no excess
Or deficit in what she breeds,
Only herself in splendid
Panoply of taste and ease.
We waste ourselves
By being blind to this.
We spend
Whole lives
Trapped within ourselves
When we can train our eyes
On things outside
And be satisfied
The sun blows,
And the moon cools,
And the hawk drives,
And the gull glides—
How much is there
That we never realize?
Is there any way
That leads us away

From self-love?
Or is life a trap
Of our own design—
A beggar's path
Through the heavy snow
That the sky throws down
To slow us in our progress
Through the ground?
Love does not know itself then,
And lust is what
Many look to find.
I cannot tell
Where all this must go:
Nature is half lust, I suppose,
But not wholly so.

CONSPIRE WITH MY HEART

I am sad tonight.
I have become a bastard
All at once,
For lack of a mother.
I lost mine somewhere
In my heart,
Or she in hers.
It makes no difference.
She is eating me
As though I were
The only thing in the desert,
My soul inflammable,
My tongue airy
And my mind sublime.
Who has a heart
In these circumstances?
Who, dear lady, knows what lies
Beneath your skin?
My heart was a garden
For me to love you in.
But you have left,
And I remain
Wandering with the nightingale
In the storm,
Trapped in the winter.
I take my chances now,
But I am never
Guaranteed to win

You back, or you me.
The wild dandelion
Will make faint wine
Once your mouth is gone
From my lips.
I rolled around the brink
Of happiness—
Love is light sometimes,
Sometimes it leaves
Us alone;
I don't like love
Much any more,
I cannot round down the score,
And you have no twin
For me to find
New pleasures in.

GLOBAL WARMING

It's getting warm.
The swallow has lost its throat
And boxes its progeny
On the ears
To make up for the problem
Of their tears.
Many are still alive
In the wilderness,
And the willows sing of fall,
Even when there is no fall.
The mussels are closing
Their lids against their fresh pain,
And turn their salty ears
Heavenward.
Warthogs roam African plains,
But slowly die out.
The world is becoming weak
In the face of modern saws.
The water-lilies float
Quietly where they can survive
In the time of little rain.
What comes down is soot and ash
In the eye; the animals
Have it—trash Nature
And you will see
How She will trash
Your progeny in her turn,
And do more than

Aggravate a dying bruise—
This is no news to anybody,
And yet it seems so.

THE CHOIR OF THE MIND

It's your brain that cannot see its nose.
My brain floats in amber glass,
Yellow diamonds surround me,
White and blue dragon-flies
Frighten me,
And the sunrise presents
A purple curtain against
The dawn.
        In the water
I can see myself questioning
Pursuit—
Values are variable,
And I am a rare duck
That makes no noise
Night or day
But only looks for a way
Out of natural perplexity:
This is a new case
And I am ambidextrous.
I speak from the past
To the current multitudes.
No one understands,
And my pain persists
Because of this.
Where does the truth go?
Is it so well hidden
That no one will ever find it?
We do not look for faith.

Just one swift idea,—
But our brains are bare,—
And a reason
Cannot be found anywhere.

PLEASANT, THE WIND

Pleasant, the wind.
I hear glass in my ears
As the air blows through them.
The pig in its sty
Is not so vulnerable
As I am.
The albatross frightens me
As it rolls by on the sea mist
Humming like a lost ghost.
I am lost in the water,
The shadow of my neck
Invisible.
I am going by now,
Engaging in my arms
The end of the world.
The pink elephants
Know as much, and have
Chosen their colors as a warning
To those who wish to resist us:
Long legs do not guarantee flight,
And fear shows no way for escape.
I know no omen
That will take you
Into the final day willingly.
You own too much
To believe in Fate,
And tomorrow you will die—

And perhaps today—
Outside the truth
Of love's domain.

A BLUE TIME

Loving you is a rapture
Of the sea.
We rest from the sun
By building pyramids of sand.
It is too soon
To say what our shadow
Does to us.
We hide behind our heads.
Life is red.
White flows down the fleshy avenue
Of the chest.
The guard-dogs bark, and
Their sense is sensual.
Look up and see the spirits fly
Out of your eyes.
You are leaving behind
Your bodies as memory.
You realize
Time will park you on the strand
With me. I am a moth
That attacks the light.
My mouth is open.
The lilies pour out
Their grief for a while.
Love's thief is gone for a while.
The mind is full of noise.
Is there poise in one finger,
Delicate as onion paper?
Do beets or greens crowd each other out
In each row?

The seed
Is very thin
Where the air blows.
Love allows love,
And shows us all the way to go.

THE TIDES

The blue in my mind
Hides my heart from you.
I am not lucky enough
To love anyone,
Much less find a love
That fits me,
Without stain.
I feel your wavy hair,
I sigh, and try to bring you near,
And you try to
Train me by degrees
To be unlike myself.
Sex is a large snake
Looking for someone to eat.
I have already tasted your ear,
Tongue and throat,
And a bit further down
On the perpendicular.
You give me a lesson
In anatomy.
Your body
Smells of smoke
And exercise. You run around me
At high speeds,
And try to push me into you.
I cannot go,
Nor can I dare say no.
I am so innocent for my age

That I would do anything but lie
To have what I crave.
You are the hope I would hang myself by.
Give me time, let me find
One not so wide at the hips
Nor florid in the nose,
Nor with so much curl
Where your dark hair grows. I prefer
Black to white,
And the night
To day.
Have we done everything,
All we had to say?
It is all we need
To keep on going
From clay to flesh
And flesh to clay.

HALLOWEEN

Handy-dandy the milkman
Deposits his milk upon
The orphanage children,
Little children running by the
Bars of the window—
Where does the mind go
When it sweeps by them
In one blow?
The able ones blow back
Upon the counter
In the ice-cream store
And hold their noses
As they pass
By the lolling trollops
On the sidewalk—
Femininity is not a crime,
Even when sold.

So the lions lie down
At peace with their souls,
And the pelicans poke
At themselves,
And the egrets stand
Upon themselves,
And the robins hop,
And the swallows
Swallow,
And a whole army

Of doves
Sweep across the
Arc of love and peace
And wish everyone
A Hallowed Evening.

REMBRANDT OR VERMEER

What's the name of the subterranean
Place left vacant
For old lace, old ladies and their silver hair,
Hand-me-downs to the activist
Heir who sports a new coiffure
For every element
That ever filled the sky
With its sight or smell?
Do we men shave ourselves
To placate nature
Or the loved one?
Are boils a plague
Of immoderation?
Do we calculate too much?
The painter is Dutch
Who gives you these scenes—
Rembrandt or Vermeer,
Or Brueghel at the inside
Of the original depiction
Of Hell. Who can tell
Where these images lead us?
Who can say
What critics will love or hate?
It is time to bake myself.
Put the poem in the oven
And turn the heat up.
We watch as our hair evaporates,
Our eyes lie wounded

On the oven floor,
Our ears turn flat
And skin registers
Enough degrees
To cook a bird's
Inviting plumage.
Love is all that is left—
Cinders into bricks
May be turned,
But this man
Has earned more than that:
Resurrection awaits the heat
Until all stain is gone,
All water skimmed
From the bone.
Then we will move from
Perpetual feud into a period
Of flaxen ease,
Helped along in wide degrees
By the tongue of truth
And love's hyperbole.

A SIP AT THE END

Play against the box.
The tiger may come out
And lick your ears
Or your tongue,
And sit down to breakfast
On your tears.
We drink only jasmine flowers
In the spring breeze
On the porch of the summer,
Late at ease.
Then the hyacinth
And the wild rose bloom,
And the cloves
Lose the bite
Of the fire
Within them.
We make soup out of tulips,
That leave an acrid taste behind.
Then we make dough to bake,
Bright with distant spices.
Love is one of them,
And we relish it together
Like a warm award
We once forgot
And, now that we are old, accept
As a tardy gift.
Tidy shoes take you to tidy places.
We never went there in our

Extended youth.
The fall has come,
And we are fighting
Within sight
Of life's last
Conundrum.

A ROUGH PASS

The laugh is in the swing
Of the arms, offering
Everything to the walker,
Who looks silently
At the sky
And determines with one eye
What the case is
And how it will turn out.
The chest heaves
And the fluid leaves
Noisily through the day,
And the doctors
Drop by and try to assess
Life's wounds, wound
Up in the patient's memory.
There is no gauge of damage
Other than the pain
Of recollection, and anticipation
Of no further sun or moon.
The feather swoons in the air
And lightly falls upon
The soul's brow, even now
When almost all that could be done
Was; a little more time
Will pass, and then we shall
Find ourselves at the end
As we expected only a few
Days ago. Before that

We were invulnerable.
But armor has a way
Of wearing thin.
It rusts,
And the will can no longer
Win the argument
The present sets for us.
There is too little oxygen,
And the eyes ooze,
And then the sky closes,
The end approaches slowly,
Almost like a baby,
Breathing in a new sleep,
On the edge of a new state,
Unsure if what is to come
Is determined by what has been.

The Lungwort and the Hellebore
: 2016 :

THE LUNGWORT AND THE HELLEBORE

For Mark Page

I'd never seen them there before,
It was as though the flowers were at war:
The lungwort and the hellebore.
But at closer sight,
It was my mind that had put
Each flower to flight,
In fact theirs was a dance
Celebrating the marriage of a prince
Of elms to a common maiden of the moss,
A match that adumbrated no loss
Of love on either side,
Lacking impediment of pride,
For love was the true metal
That sent every petal
On its flight along the ground:
Love makes a sound
That even the deaf can hear,
So don't close up your ear,
The flowers are speaking to you very near.

(N.B.: In reading, I pronounce "Hellebore" as "Heeleebore" in ignorance of any lexical authority.)

MISTER APOLLO

My soul moves
Me beyond words;
My soul is stretched
In heaven beyond
Your wandering
Eye, the eye
That never saw
Me in you,
That lost me
As I sang to the trees,
Turning leaves
With my breath.
I wonder what is left
Of the red salamanders
We spotted on the spring road,
Mating?
There was space in nature
For us, but you chose
To live alone,
And now I see
No one in my room,
The enormous flowering room
Of my loveliness.

SUMMER SUNFLOWERS

They buffet the wind,
Circling in the freeze,
The blue jay,
The downy woodpecker
And the chickadees.
My mother looks
Through the kitchen window
And sees their rivalry
For her seeds,
Summer sunflowers,
Dried and now
Cracked on the snow.

Who knows the cold
Better than these?
Better than my mother?
Better than me?

VISITING TIME

There is still time to come.
The nurse wants to speak
With you, the parent,
To turn us
Around.
Not everyone
Has this chance.
Take words:
They fly
And we try to hear.
They are too short,
And we talk
And our nerves
Speak.
We place ice
On our wounds.
We look at the weather
Inside and say:
"Try to take the words away.
Take us, too.
We love our words
For a while,
Then we go."

WHERE AM I?

Someone has come back.
It is me.
I have fallen
Into reality,
A strange place.
I am a foreigner here.
I swear.
I pick up the furniture
And throw it around.
That feels good
At first.
Then it hurts.
And I am still here.
The days dog me.
I have been over-sleeping
For a long time.
I do not hear myself whine.
I am fine.
I was once lost
As a gully bird
Or a snip in the sea.
Now I am me.
I still wish
I were somewhere else.
But there isn't anywhere else
To be.

SOCRATES' APOLOGY

I want to write another poem,
With a picture in it,
Of a dolphin or a squared
Hypotenuse, or the backbone
Of a whale, or a house
On fire
At Christmas, looking
Red in the light snow,
Glowing as its life
Goes out in the darkness.
The hypotenuse of the triangle
Is not red,
It is alone;
It has lost its two angles,
Two extremes,
And all that remains
Is an empty line
Floating on the page
Of a mathematician's dark
Mind, blind out of obedience
To someone else's eye.
Now we can have no triangles,
And geometry
Is suffering,
And someone is
Dictating what comes next in line,
Like the purple swale,
Or the black swan.

One full soul is witness to this,
But you can't find him now;
He left here a long time ago,
And he won't come back
Even for an apology.

The snow is deep,
The gravel cracks
Beneath the tired windowsill,
The voices of men can be heard inside
Discussing things.
It is important to understand
Birds, and the swale,
And the black swan.
The night is gathering them
Into its folds,
As the men try to find
A way out.

The body is light to the touch
Though weighty to see and hold.
Can we blame the blind
For what they do not see?
The deaf for what they do not hear?
The dead for their ignorance?
We cry, and
Our amber tears flow.
Turn us over on our toes
So we can walk away exposed
To the usual elements.

THE PEACH TREE GROWS

The peach tree
Send its labors
Into its roots;
Above ground,
There is sweet juice
For bees and wasps
And me and you
And the tantalized baby
I once was,
Looking out the window
At the tree,
My tree,
With no idea
One day soon it
Would not be there.
Someone has delivered
It in pieces
To another place,
I suppose with the bees
And a wasp,
And its soul broken
On the back
Of its leaves,
If a peach tree
Could be said ever
To have harbored
Some divinity.

THE DOVE AND I

I am licking licorice
Over your face,
And I am dripping signs
Of love all over
Your body, where
You feel my eyes
Eat you up.
I measure myself
By you, and I think
In the dark sometimes
That wine and a piece
Of your bread
Will keep us going.

I think too much,
Like a waterfall,
And you spin
Underneath me
Lying on your back
To show your claws.
I am hiding behind you,
And introduce myself.
You look up at me
And say hello again,

And the water
Falls on my face
Until I let go
For the first time

And every time after that:
You, the dove, once said
To me—
But now I do not hear you,

You have fallen into the spirit
Of the fall,
I cannot call
You back,

Your wings have turned black,
Your place in the wood is a blank.
The truth is—
Your eye is on the rose,
And your neck
Bending over me
Allows my eyes to close.

ADVENT

Write each scene
As though it were a life,
Make life art,
Discrepancy aside.
Put the risk
Into the choice,
The unexpected love,
The sigh of sighs;
Advance the heat—
Our love's complete,
The pain is gone
As we go by.

WHAT THEY DIDN'T WANT

The small family
Smells the dark
Of the empty farmhouse,
Living above the eggs
In the cellar,
And the old woman there
With her candle,
Looking for blood.
The eggs will go out
To the inns
And the fresh kitchens,
Where menus are made
To order for the hungry
Of all estates,
Afraid of the depths
And the heights,
Disrobed in both,
As though rich and poor
Could be hungry for
The same food,
More than they can eat
Before they die
Of the greatest hunger
They can know,
That they carry around
In their throats, wailing
Beyond the eggs,

Beyond the shell
That breaks,
Beyond the crown
No one ever gave to them,
That couldn't come to them
Without their wanting it.

PAINTING A LADY

If I keep writing
About you,
You may become famous.
What will I then be?
I am sticking my face
In yours,
So I can't breathe
While you laugh.
Then I hang onto
Your neck.
You bend and I fall,
Like a gull.
Love can taste good.
I ate mind yesterday,
And today
I am swimming in ink.
My eyes are tired of writing,
But it is my job
To create something
Nice for the ladies.
They have their souls, too,
And were taught
Not to make a scene.

OFF WE GO

I've got to wear the brown ones.
Otherwise,
I will be a cripple
On the right
Before night.
After nine,
It's alright again,
Because then
I am writing about
You and our love
That just went past
So quickly
I am still in pain.
That is love,
Up to his tricks.
I enjoyed
The non-existent kisses,
And watching you eat
Fish, and crumbling
My toast in your craw.
And then there are always
The Italian restaurants,
And the Greek,
And the cheap Chinese ones.
They have gone past, too.
And I am left with you.
I remember one day
When I told you
About the greatest pain

I had ever suffered,
And it was about love.
And you have given
Me that pain again,
Like a surprise.
My little love has died.
My little love.
And you
Are immaculate forever.

A MYSTERY SLOW TO BE REALIZED

It's a gift.
I sit on the hotel bed
And read the roses
Printed on the pillow.
I am a hybrid,
And what I read
Startles me, as though
I were already dreaming
Of my last love,
Which came through
An open window
In spring, when I was
Guarding my life
As though
The slightest whisper,
At the least expected moment,
Would wipe us all away,
As though *fama infama*
Would crawl by our shadowy feet
Unseen,
And kill our joy.
The doves have built
Their nest in my window again,
And the squirrels have taken
Their eggs again and left
The birds bleak and hollow.
Squirrels are rats with tails
And will eat the bark off trees

At the end of the winter.
I am in mourning for the doves,
And I think their loss
Is hidden only for a while
In the mystery of nature.

BLESSING

That's a very nice jacket,
And I'm glad to have it,
A present from you,
Running red wild over my shoulder.
Everyone is so explicit
About love!
I hide mine in my
Suit with you.
I walk carefully,
And sound like I am singing
When I ought to be serious.
Somebody is in a calamity
About me
But we hide so well
That no one hears or reads
What we say or do.
There is no hope
For our sole body.
The familiar keeps intervening
Between us,
Lacking mystery
As though we really were lovers,
But we aren't.
We smile,
And make each other laugh,
And that is enough for me,
Since if you understood

The risk you run
You would fold up your chair
And get out of the way completely.

WE WALK DOWN THE STRAND

Maybe no poem will
Come to me today.
Maybe the lines
Waiting for bread
And water are lengthening.
There are rats in the beer,
And the sun is overflowing,
And it is still
Hard to see.
The ambulance has carried away
The man dying,
And shortly his body
Will be empty.
Then the ravens will have their day, too,
And the unjust will flourish.
Desire is a wan carrier
And inexplicable.
We walk down the strand
Under the overcast sky,
And somewhere, a man
Is saying a rosary
Not in church,
But in memory
Of something kind
And unexpected,
Of a person
Who opened up
All the closed doors

And found applause
Amongst all
The new nations.

THE INJURED EYE

What is the matter
With my injured eye?
Why can't I touch
Your hips with mine?
My head
Is falling out of you,
My hair is let out
On the ground,
And abandon takes over
Between my legs.
I am teaching myself
To be wild and old.
I am learning
To whistle with spotted teeth,
Separated with gaps in my breath,
Leaning over the ice
Of my approaching end.
There is still a laugh in me,
And my lips are bright.
They rattle, and
My tongue rolls,
My feet tie me
To the ground,
Or I would
Fall completely over the edge.
I try to smooth
My rough neck
With oil, and my swelling nose

Spoils my face.
There are holes
Where I used to place
Words.
My eyes are cold.
My last bed is beginning
To shake,
And the laurel
Has fallen from my head.
No door opens away
From all this,
Except to let air escape
Through the cracked throat.
Grant me a wish,
And I will ask
That everyone else
Be denied this.

THEY DON'T KNOW

They don't know
How to kill me.
It could be
With my breath,
Or the depth
Of my soul,
Or the sign
Of some truth
On my head.
It could even be
Through love,
Which they try
To sell to me
All the time.
But my heart
Is not willing
To die for them.
So they try to arrange
Things for themselves.
And I watch
The winter turn
Slowly to spring.
My winter
Will turn, too,
I know it will,
Even if I love you.
There are many
Prologues possible
In this world,

And you
Are one of them.
I am feeding
Them.
One day some of them
Will die despite
My attention.
The rest will make up
My family,
And we will beat
The hateful ones
Out of existence.
We will just
Wait for them,
And out
They will go.
The show will be splendid,
And we will tie our shoes
With our patience.
Then we will walk on.

PHILOSOPHY

Philosophy
Is the curse
Of those who don't know
But would like
To find out.
But
I don't like
Your philosophy.
In fact,
I prefer talking
To the birds
On the beach.
I make them fly away
With my sounds,
But they come back
To me
And the tides.
My hand is in their face
For a while,
But they know
Their time is running out
And mine is not.
They are running out
Of choice about
Where to find eternity.
Maybe
They will give it to me.
Maybe they will turn

Their backs on me.
Maybe they will fill
The sand
With their heads.
If I go,
They will be
All alone,
And I will
Be with them.

A GRAVE SITUATION

Have you got me now?
Have you got me nailed?
Am I hanging
In front of your
Dirty eyes,
Explaining my pain?
When will you get
Tired of me?
When will you stop?
How great is the power
Of hate?
I am lying
On the floor
In my first role.
In my first role
I am dead
Throughout the play
And I am not
Allowed to say
Anything.
Then the audience
Goes away.
I think this is the play
Of my life
And that it
Will never end.

Who will come out
To play with me now?
Outside it is raining.
Inside, I am boxed up
On the floor
In my grave.
Is there anything
Left to save?

SNOW

There is a little hint of it,
But nothing serious,
Just a tear,
A nose blown,
A ragged eye.
The mouth moves
Silently, and the
Whole chest cries
Inside, like a tomb
For a lost love,
Fresh wretched love,
Promise gone.
Birds do not fall
Out of love,—
Or other animals,—
Breeding underneath
The canopy of the warm
Summer. Once bred,
They all
Go south, and their love
With them.
The thin winter stays,
With a few stray birds,
Or a squirrel:
They count days
As the wind rises
Over the whole lawn
Of life,

And blows the snow
In their eyes,
Hiding their hearts for some,
For the next summer,
If there is one.

FLOATING ON THE WATER

Did the white swan
Get that feeling
On its own
Floating on
The water, racing
To see
Who could be first?

Some stay on the shore,
Hiding from the water.

I am listening
When I am supposed
To be sleeping,
And the white swan
Is listening with me,
And we talk together.

You would not believe it,
But color
Has nothing to do
With the night,
It is all about
The extreme
Cold.

The swan and I,
We float in the water
And we are calm.
We do not judge
Our pain.

We listen to the dogs
Bark,
And watch the
Butterfly
Try to escape
The flower,

Defenseless,
And then
We turn to you
And ask
What have we done
With the water,
With the rain,
That you hate us so?

INTEMPERATE WEATHER

I'll get it if I need it.
I do need light,
But suffer
The bite
Of the dark.
Are we afraid again?
Are we afraid
For us
Or for others?
You have eyes.
Do you distribute lies?
That is why
For years
I have been
Tripping over the souls
Of the abandoned.
They and I
Will die together
Before our day
Really gets started.
The morning is wet.
I cannot hear
A bird.
The wind is slack.
The toads
Are croaking again.
There is movement

Now in the news—
I cannot take you
Anywhere forever.

IN HAWAII

In Hawaii,
There you go swimming
In the wave with the fish
And the centaur
And the snapdragon
That floats on your nose
As though it could never
Find its own end,
On your nose,
As the wind
Blows through you
Horizontal in the water,
Flying past the termagants
And gully birds,
And the sea snips.
You make great food
In your short suit,
Playing games with
The birds. You take
Their claws seriously,
And put the skies away.
You even play
With me sometimes,
Especially when I look
At that suit
Between your legs.
I mean to capitalize
On you, if I can.

But you are improvident,
And wave me away
Horizontally, and my heart
Goes blank in the wind,
And my nostrils blow
Wildly in the shadow
Of the bright blue Hawaiian sky,
And I lie in my bed by myself
And wonder
How could I have done
All this with you—
And still
Live alone?

A SINGLE SUMMER

In memory of youth at Keewaydin

Love lies a little,
And its limits fall
Beyond the heat
Down to the soil.
The irises in the fields
Reflect upon themselves,
As the purple gentian
Parts the grass,
And the small orange and yellow
Poles of Indian paintbrush
Color the new field
A summer meadow.
The robin has arrived
With the spring
And pokes for worms
And feeds it fledglings.
The doves bend their necks
In the salty road;
Who sees these
By the wood?
We sit down
Upon the summer's skirt,
Listening.
The tree is hollow,
And the fern interrupted
By its spore.

Where does power flow
Beneath their stems'
Faint breath?
Why the stealth,
The self-inwardness?
We can already
Smell the rain.
We lie
On the blue lawn
And drink,—
And think of what
Nature offers
And endures.
This is the story
Of one day
In the North
That no word from anyone
Can wash away or spoil.

THE BOOK

And the poet
Came and went.
He put down his struggle
To madness,
Watering the iris
In the window box,
And the tulips in love,
And the summer.
The squirrels
Recorded his presence
With their tails,
And with his smile
He recorded their riches
As though all they stole
Would one day
Go back
To its owners.
But once the spirit goes,
It does not come back.
It starts on a different journey
That the priests
And the poets
Say they have tasted.

While we wait,
We lead a good life.

Once we were awake.
There is no sound now.

Only the lapping
Of our lips
As we put down the book
At its end
And wonder
If we would like
To try it again.

VISIONS OUT OF AFRICA

I can write a poem
Of any shape, large
Like an elephant
Nosing through the bush
Or a giraffe,
Eating tempting trees,
Or an orangutan
Wheezing in the fold,
Or the wild ostrich,
Racing nowhere
With its head down low,
And the pink
Flamingo,
At the corner of the sea,
Floating,
And the horny tree-toad
That mates with a blast
From its black throat
At the base
Of the banyan tree.
All of Africa
I hear and see,
A poem filling out
Everything but the human.
And where are we?
I think we have disappeared
Into the past,
Along with the most recent

Generals and politicians,
With their visions—
But I can't tell
What they see
Here or in Africa,
Because
They can't tell
Me.

THE GIFT

Life is what I do to myself
And to you;
Then you do it to me
And yourself,
And your giving
And mine
Amplify
The sound
Of everyone living.

IRAQ COMPOS MENTIS

Where will they put me
When I am done?
Why does everyone
Carry around
A small litter
Of bones,
The same small
Jewels, false imagery,
Prized by
Fashion, cheap
To touch?
We keep our counsel
Light as an empty sword,
Guarding an empty door,
One eye, looking
For its reflection
Upon the ground.
I see rivalry
Between mates,
Brothers hating each other,
Vexation moving
Hearts to commit
Themselves to crimes
Before anyone
Can judge them.
What tune do teeth
Press to your ears?
Where is the reed

That lies
Upon your lips? Whose notes
Would you blow
Over your head
Into the kind atmosphere?
The rain would stop,
If you would let it.
Ceremony would have meaning
Again—it would not drown
In your spite.
My love has gone
Out the door.
There are no more willing
Hearts to ply.
The little pains of age appear
As time runs near.
Who has brought you back?
Why have you come
To disturb us?
We are unwilling witnesses
To the rise
Of impromptu anarchy.
Age falls down
Into the grave,
And the young
Lack all foresight.
The wise are unbound,
And the bonds between
Us break as though
Care had unraveled care.

Take quick stock
Of what you have done.
The lifeless are left behind,
And day drags after day.
The nights need love
But cannot find it.
The trees stand round
Their dry demise,
And the tongues
Of passion pour
Disdain upon its enemies.
Shame evaporates,
And the art
Of amity freezes
On the sill.
The start of life itself
Closes, and there are
No more cries
Of any kind of hope left.
We bind our ears,
And the truth moves
More slowly than the armies
Of the day. There is no way
To avoid slaughter.
All innocents die,
And to survive
Is a trick
Few wits can master
As few can master wit.
Try to turn left or right.

There is nothing there.
Drink grief—
And see the eye of war
Stare down love,
That cannot endure
The weight we place on it.
Stone will float
Through the air
Before we find
The other side of pain.
One day words will
Return our compliments,
And lovers lie in bed satisfied.
The interim is wary of its bounds,
And moves too slowly
To succeed completely
In its work.
Praise patience
And avoid the Good,
And some better day
Than this will come.

Now wash your hands in brine:
Your years cannot come clean.
You parade your heart
In the dark
In front of us,
And I am not pleased
With your touch.
We cannot walk back

Except in memory,
And few love what
They never knew.
There is a picture of
You in my head,
Standing over the dead
Light.
I can hear the tread
Of armies
In front of me.
I see the breath
Of thousands of souls
Opened to take in air,
Bodiless.
I tell them
That they left too soon,
That I loved them—
That the dove fell unwillingly.
I see its white shadow
Lift,
And you propose a toast to impotence
And lies,
And suckle the pigs that crawl
On the rotten floor
Of the world.
There is little to say
To them.
Sometimes my mind
Floats in and out of my mouth,
But no words come,

And bitter streams of thought
Rattle down my throat.
White sheets light
The sky, and the surviving souls
Ask why there is no sun,
And I reply:
"Put your hats on, men
Of trade. Cover yourselves
With gold,
And live on what you earn.
Deny the poor.
Rape the women
Of your choice.
Call the innocent to account
And lock them up.
Place the weak apart.
Assassinate the insane.
They have no rights.
They cannot fight you,
And there will always be
An empty heart willing
To kill for you.
What is ahead?
I propose nothing.
You can do no wrong,
And I cannot speak—
Only—
The whole world moves near to extinction
Because of you.
There are no eyes

On your altar tonight;
See the picture of pain above
That comes down
So far.
Turn your bloated face
Towards your shame:
Watch your teeth rot,
Your eyes go blind,
Your ears close tight
Against the wave
Of wailing wrongs.
Your hair burns,
And your fingers
Lose their touch.
Your soul stinks
Of burning flesh,
And your war's sword
Will cut off your head
In the end.
Until then
You gain the day,
And lies
Give you cover
For the next
Round of abuse.
You try to use me.
Who faces you down?
You know you will
Never count the end
Of my pain.

One day death
Will eat you and throw
Up your remains
On the dry plain.
Try to survive one more day of this,
And you will find
The price of life
Is too high: love
Will take you down
For perpetuity—
And so will I."

WHAT THE FOOL COULD TELL

What the fool saw in truth
Was himself,
With a spot on his soul,
For all that he had missed
And could never tell.

THEN THE FULL LOVE

In this perfect world,
We would eat blueberries
And our tongues would not be stained;
We would blow kisses in winter,
And our lips would not freeze;
In summer, we would hang on the alder
And its leaves would not tremble;
We would bear children
And we would not cry.
Someplace deep,
We feel our love divide
And rise, conquering
The whole body,
Back up to the lips,
Which we bite,
As though for the first time
Learning what we
Can never forget,
Even in age,
And never regret,
Still together.

GRASS

Slide along the blade:
Grass is tame and wild
By turns
And must cut throughout
With art
As a garden
Within itself,
Painted on the ground.

HARVEST

The soldier moss stands
At attention in the rain
As star moss covers the wet terrain
Beneath the trees,
And grounded ferns feel the breeze,
Even the interrupted fern,
Which spends its spore
Thriftily, its gift
To man and nature.
Bears plunder the wild blueberries
In fields where fire has passed
And offered nutrients to the soil.

Summer stalks the garden:
Early radishes sprout,
Tomatoes crowd each other out,
Angry at their stakes
For pulling them back
From wandering at will
Amongst the thyme and dill.

Such summer luxury turns to fall,
When hay fails the bobolink,
The meadowlark turns south,
And the dread of frost
Spreads its white chill
Against the garden wall.

The Name We Never Lose
: 2016 :

KILL ME NOW

When people try to give me tests
They always fail.
I don't know why; they are shortening
Their lives unduly.
It's like baking a soufflé
That falls.
The sky falls and the rain falls,
And none of us will see his soufflé again.

I wish I were not alone with the rain.
It is easier to laugh with someone.
A guide, perhaps, smelling of
French cherries and cinnamon.
Or a baker, who feeds
His pastries to the geese.

Will you be my guide?
Beyond the rain and the geese,
The cherries and webbed feet?
Will you kiss me?

Or kill me now
Before I lie,
Before I have to falsify
Who I am and how I've died
A thousand times beneath your eye.

WHAT MY LOVE WILL SEND TO ME

First, he will send me his eyes,
So that I may see him in the dark;
Next he will send me his mouth,
So that I may speak with him in tongues;
Third, he will send me his lips,
So that I may kiss him;
Fourth, he will send me his ears,
So that I may hear the world moan
As we roll together;
Fifth, he will send me his hair,
So that I may touch something fine;
Then he will send me his soul,
So that I may know him whole;
Seventh, he will send me his heart,
So that we cannot be apart:
Time will send us the rest,
By which he and I will be blest.

UNDERGROUND

Slight and sly,
The worm slips
Beyond my eye:
I try to find his hole
And come up with a mole.
Like the worm,
The mole lives beneath the surface
Of the wave,
He hides outside the scope of everyday,
Unless you think
The quotidian exists
A foot below
The grass and leaves
That other creatures
Find adequate for summer ease.

KISS, KISS

Fight for love?
Not me.
I'm perfectly pain-averse.
Your concern hurts.
I can see you coming.
I'm into singularity.
It's my own home.
I am about to turn blue—forever.
Then you will remain
Completely imaginary,
Like a crack in the dark.

DECEMBER

December, month of ice,
Black cold, black device,
Tell me why you lie upon my eyes
So quietly. I think
You sleep peacefully,
Preparing me—
Am I to live again,
And rise from the ice and snow
And smell once more
The hyacinth,
The honeysuckle and the rose?
December, do not toy
With me. Leave me in peace
If life cannot come twice.
I think, in any case,
I would sooner die once
for all,
Than turn more than once
to ice.

THE ARCHBISHOP IN SPITE OF HIMSELF

A tone down the corridor
Echoes the eye, the sense of what we see

Lies on the mind, pale next to the sun,
A shade. The heliotrope blooms,

And we turn to the red and say,
'How easy it is to be red'.

The red is what we have made,
And the heliotrope, as we saw it,

Was made, was made red,
And so on. This is when

We are this side of night;
At night the heliotrope turns blue,

The stars are white, and the sky
An even distance from the eye.

That, too, is what we make it,
Though what we make ourselves

Is ambiguous: out of our
Imagination, we imagine ourselves

As a metaphor for what we sense:
Warmth in the wind and air the color of absinthe.

AND FOR DESSERT...

Some people want the bomb,
but are perplexed because
they cannot find it anywhere.

Look under your chair, warrior,
you are missing a leg or two,
and if you get that damn bomb,
there will be no more of you.

THE NAME WE NEVER LOSE

I send my soul out
To be cleaned.
It does not mean anything
Before I wash
It in brine
And look to sand
To rub out all imperfections
Of being that I usually
Don't detect. I am tired
Of looking within.
I have exhausted
The spring with planting;
Now I must scrape
What I can from the seams
Of the earth that lie
Beneath my feet, hardened
By summer heat
And my own dead weight.
I am not free
To go away from myself.
Place me where you like,
Inside the dark or not,
It is no use:
I see the frame of the world
From where I stand,
And I await its interesting fate —
Fortune is too late
To blink. My enemies
Die intestate

And I seize their remains.
Love of God
Got them release beneath the earth
They walked on.
Their bare bodies bristle
As I pass over them.
One day I shall be buried
In the moon or in a place
Further away where I
Have not been
For a long time.
I was once young there,
And stayed
For a while.
Now that I have a decided
Age, I have learned
To live apart,
And dispose honestly
Of my war's dubious spoil.
All goods flow about me now,
I am liberated into the arms
Of friends, new memories
And a long past.
Expectation has grown
Into fact, and love ceases
To take its toll of me.
I tip forward,
And find I can move
Obstacles inside me that once
Were enough to keep me still.

Turn me once, you love-sick
Of history.
Life is like the sea —
Everything empties into it,
And nothing leaves,
— Except the pure mist.
We think we have won the war,
But we only lose
What we never know. And
What has come,
Has already gone before.

HIPPOCRATES

I will write one more,
To make it five.
The same as
My maximum daily number
Of orgasms.
Imagination is not cheap,
And orgasm is dear.
And crudity in poetry
Has its precedents.
Even truth can obtrude
In the strangest places.
I think I am unwanted
Here or there.
Remember Hippocrates:
Do no harm,
And the patient may survive.
I shall write one more,
To make it five.

DIBBLE-DABBLE

Dibble-dabble,
Dibble-dabble,
It's me you meet
Upon your plate,
It's me you eat
Without compunction
Or regret.
Someday,
Our positions will reverse,
And then reverse again,
And we will spend eternity
Eating each other without end.

SUMMERTIME

Dry ice on a wet lawn—
  Freezing grass in the rain
Makes it hard to provide the mice
  With a haircut.
The moles are subaqueus
  And escape the cold,
And the worms are pink,
And the crickets leap in the leaves
And make love in the evening
  Underneath the windows
Where everyone can hear them—
  I wish I were a cricket
In the summertime,
  But then I would not live long.
Such are the penalties of copulation.

TROUBLE

I am waiting:
Give me tongue,
And you shall hear
The revolution
Of the spheres:
The word has neighbors
Everywhere,
In the atmosphere
And out—
I know the trouble
You're about.

PEARLS

Pearls lie deep
Beneath the gray-back swell,
Or fall like tears
Into a weeping well,
Evanescent as the breath
Of the moon's white sphere,
They light the ocean's crest
Like moonbeams
Dressed in air.

TRYING TO HIDE?

Trying to hide?
In my lap?

That's a red venue
For Puritans.

You can stay there
As long as you

Don't shake.
I do not solicit

Vibrations.

TWINS

       i.
In the corner of my room,
Sits my eye.
It recognizes me in the evening
When the light dies.
It is not connected to anything.

       ii.
What a pain knowledge is.
It is as though someone
Had let the devil out
To watch us
And we had to cause trouble
So he would have a purpose.

       iii.
My other eye sees this,
But says nothing.
It is afraid of annihilation,
Which is going to come anyway,
So why not be brave
And face it?
Face it down,
And one day
We will have both our eyes back
Working for us
Facing down death,
Like the good eyes they are.

APPLE TRIP

What do we see in Apple?
The glorification of tree?
A seed for future use?
Present delicacy?

We have no tongue,
And our teeth are masticating
A past with no name:
What an appetite to tame!

We have left our friends behind.
They were not friends anyway.
Silence told us so.
Silence is a sign
My friends cannot read.
They just give it to me—
The usual human development.

"I built a temple all of gold
That none did dare to enter in."

It is light inside,
Even for those without glasses.

I try to speak so carefully!
And I give you a headache:
Try death. It is without headaches.
It is your commencement.

You take your degree
And move into a good neighborhood.

Do you still have time to kill?
Are you wading on the beach
By the murmuring sea?
Can you float onomatopoetically?
You are like a new bond
Or some other security.
Or are you counterfeit?

I know you are in the funds.
Your pain is in the wings.
Try them, and you will see
Farther into the heart of me
Than my own perfectibility.

OTHER

You will use my madness
To give me pain — you,
Who speak in the guise of truth
And wish me ill.
Have I not pain enough
For ten of you, or twenty?
Can you really be invulnerable?

You have given me the gift of my faults.
I have already lived with them,
They know me,
And I have made them my friends.
It is as if I lived with them
On a small island and we passed
Our time shifting places.

I am now all that I have been
And shall be,
History and potentiality.
My faults cannot destroy me.
Nor my madness.
Nor you.

PRIMUS INTER PARES

First Grade:

I'll never forget the four flights up
    my first day,
And the tall blond Amazon winging down
    eight flights my way,
Forcing me to choose
    right or left, I could not say.
I stood still, wondering if
    I could obey:

Then I smiled and shyly realized
    That I was free,
Since I could choose my Amazon,
    And my Amazon, me.

A PLANGENT TEAR

You ask me
To write a line.
From it fly
Pink sighs, blue tears
And yellow apostrophes.
A great freeze
Is hanging in the air:
Three weeks
Defined by a dry tear.

It fits, this sound.
I smell my enemies dying.
We love each other more now.

NAKED FOR A DAY

Time to dine? Nonsense.
I am not proper.
I have fallen out
With ambiguity.
Here I am,
Naked for a day,
Lolling without appetite.
Blood is hasty,
But my knife is empty.
Can your tongue be far behind?

VERTICAL ALERT

i.

An eye's body alive.
That's what arms us.
Then we are ready
For the piccolo,
For the final note
Before combat.

ii.

Where are we at?
Honey, you tell me.
I'm jes climbin'
Them stairs
To eternity,
An' there ain't
No one gonna
Knock me off,
Even the stairs the'selves,
Jus' 'cause they's tricky.
On'y God gets all the way up.
An' he's stuck;
So I say,
Heave him ova
The hump
An' we'll all get home.

ODE TO WATER

Wherefore worry?
I am indulgent
Blue spruce, my love,
We are in the same basket.

This white planet
Is my subject,
But I am not its lord.
We are mutual communicants,
And dry and therefore white.

Where did we find ourselves out?
In the bath—quite a lie.
There are three things to remember from this:
(1) Don't forget to breathe;
(2) Remain still but vulnerable;
(3) Accept the love you can return.

Love is a pin that pricks.
And so on.
If you have a chair, don't use it for kindling:
Sit on it.
Even I freeze. It is best to be
Seasonally adjusted.

Keynes would have loved you,
His pitch is so sincere,
His mind mundane,

We observe him in parts,
Seeing what we wish to see.

The red moon is mounted
On a Keynesian base—
It has its cycles.
It pedals along,
Filling in the troughs
And mounting hills—
Why not be creative?

Well, water, come, I shall ask you:
How can I hide?
Where is the W.C.?

SELF DELIVERY

Abuse my nerves!
They will fall on you.
I am an intricate web
Of consistency.
Flies catch me,
And I eat them up.
Down is another direction.
You will see this
When you falsify yourself for the
Last time.
Even armor-plate won't
Help you—it will lock you
Inside your problem.
You need care
Of every description.
What can you do?
What do you do?
Whatever it is,
Live on it.
It will deliver you.

ALABAMA IN PAINTING

Entirely too blue, you see, she said,
Other colors count too,
Some even expand with their meanings
If you breathe them quickly.
Monster hopes are quick to reduce
With a sigh from white—
That is clean—and then we
Feel not what we imagine,
But what is there.

Yellow is the illumination of the
Universe, and travels around without
Apparent locomotion—it is
A queen, born to lead,
And it does so sweetly,
And discretely, even in
Shadow time.

Amber is yellow's cousin, and
Draws us into the shade.
That is the ease we need.

Brown is clean, also, though
It is the dirt's color.
But look who lives in the dirt!
Snakes and salamanders
And maiden-hair ferns,
Lichens and soldier moss,
All live in the shade.

Black is the negative number.
Is it death?
No, it is nothing, which anything
Can become.
Red is love, which anything
Can become.

We are beginning to understand
Those. Let us fix our understanding
Gently.
Are you arranged for green?
Yes, it is youth and anything new.
It requires useful instruction
Dutiful patience and care.
It is not without work,
But you will find in the end
That it will repay you all your love.

OPUSCULAR THOUGHTS

Opuscular thoughts through
Oracular words work
Miraculous deeds with
The dead.

The live are the dead,
They lack heart, soul or head,
They have only a corpse,
(We have only remorse),
And they pour all their tears
Into infinite years
Of dear penury.

FELINE MAINTENANCE

My cat understudies
A dragon in disguise,
So don't cross his tracks
Or he'll kill you with his eyes.

COLOR ROLE

Blue will teach you
What is sin,
Red alludes to what's within,
Green is youth
And black the dark,
Brown the home of horny bark.
If you wish to know still more,
You must knock on love's back door.
Open it and look within,
There you'll see your crimson skin,
Luring men to strange demise,
Beyond the practice of their eyes.

A SHORT TRANSLATION

This can go there, and that, too.
Tell me, do you weep at particles?
Greek verbs do it most often:
A little jog of syntax
Sets them off.
The professors don't understand.
But they translate anyway,
Like the moon across the sky,
Only the moon arrives.
And the professors?
They don't translate
Like you and I.

DOUBT

Beauty is the beast we all long for.
Wealth hides wrinkles within the exterior,
A fold or two in fame will still attract
A youth willing to bed an artifact.

Put the outside in,
Do not give up,
What nature will not give,
Fantasy offers as reprieve.

WORKING OUT PARALLELS

Someone I know is
Hero of the pick-up,
Has dirty ears that don't hear,
Eyes that wipe reality
Out of existence, see
Substantial debt stateside,
And international recklessness.

We may reach very far
Into the stratosphere,
But is that Heaven?
It used to be, seen from here,
Until we went through it.
Now we are condemned
To contemplate the Universe.

Is it Heaven?
Somewhere we lost our future.
The truth can be highly beguiling,
Until it changes.
I am willing to change you,
If you are willing, too.
Life moves, and sometimes we are
Sitting on top of it.

NAKED

It is probably the time
That makes me cry,
It is like love and
Needs no name.

Beyond apocalypse
Is the end we don't
Anticipate.

It is sweetness. I should
Look forward to this.
My mind runs backward
To the beginning:
I am swimming
In dreams, an empty wind
Unveiling itself before the world
As audience, unashamed.

OBLIGATO

I'll start verso obligato,
Racing horses in my mind,
I cannot climb beyond my reason,
Seasoning will not cure this poison,
I am drowning in smoke,
Pale fires outlive me
As if to testify to suicide.
Enrich my history as you like,
I am a take between
Two tables; I run along
Like a young child,
Heedless. I will never
Eat the pear on the pear-tree,
Or the apricot or the apple;
The ice is dry that holds you lifeless
By the phlox and marigold.

PROLIXIN

Parlay your tongue
Into a weapon of war.
Turn the stone over
And crawl underneath
To find the slug's hiding place
And your soul's
Own darkness.
We are treading on our toes
As lightly as ballerinas
In the summer dusk.
They arrive too late
At the front door.
Time is closed now.
And the way out through the mouth
Is gone. The delectable
Light is flying by
You without a greeting.
You have yet to choose your end.
Let me only depress your tongue
With my aid
And you will fall mute
Into the final crisis.

A HARD RAP

Will you tell
The Guest to depart?
Love is unwelcome
In Elktown
And sex is sold:
the people could all be born
Of little seeds
In the ground,
And grow up wolves.
How is the soul conceived?
Outside time.
Some of us die
Without one.
It is a long way to go
For nothing.

MY NOCTURNAL MIGRATIONS

Your eyes are marble eyes,
They are fixed with grey striations
Moving across two small expanses.
I move, too,
From one eye to two,
Afraid of the penalty
Of abjuration.
I will keep my mouth closed
In the shape of a rose,
Growing along the path
I have chosen.
What will is there?
What courage?
I must learn to row
Beyond the limits of a good name.
What I think is private
Unless you hear me do it
And see the sense behind it.
I am sure you will expose me
If I drop my eyes.
I am paralyzed by good behavior.
Sooner or later I may surrender
To my enemies
And bring them down.
I sweep daily,
And hope for a future occupation.
I don't think I can face death
Demonized.

THE MIRROR AND THE MASK

Will you accept the blank difference
Between one and one, this and that

Two measurables? We make things to measure
So that we may know them, as

The blue tapestry at Verdun,
Or Grandmother's black coffee table,

A new measure imposing a revolution
On past ponderables,

Leaving Verdun at one with the present
Of history. Blank materialists will laugh with Lenin:

They know what they know
And turn things upside down.

Then we see as in a mirror what we were
And are. Only the mask is different.

A MILLION SPOTS

The artist slides,
And speckles, too,
A spot along
A million—two.

Inspection
Of my head I see
And wonder
What is wrong with me:

There's nothing new
That I can see,
I watch you, too,
As you watch me.

BUYING NOTHING

The dime will buy you nothing,
Except two nickels or ten pennies,
A small range of change
Available to any beggar in the street,
If he accepts dimes;
And if he does,
Is it strange
Should he reject the possibility of
Change?

A ZEN STATE

I write by looking away
From the mark.
I move by indirection.
The eye leads away from
What is seen,
From imperfect to perfect
    imperfection.

Odd,
That what I see
I haven't got,
And what I have
I cannot see:
There is more than simple perplexity
In this for me.

LUCRETIA LOCUPLES

Writing is another country,
A country without a name:
A lily is its outer face,
Its inner face a flame.

LEIDER

Our Nemesis is
an apple dumpling
in the fog—
A large decision
coming around
the corner.

REVENGE

I am not supposed to be writing poetry,
I am supposed to be turning up my nose
And taking revenge.

But where my nose is going
There is no air,
And revenge is not possible.
There is enough revenge already.

I wish it were spring again,
And even that the rain would come
And clean us up.
I need a wash.
I think a lot, and a wash
Would make me feel better.

I can hear mice
Coming out of the woodwork.
They live there in winter
And come out at night
Looking for food.
The cat eats them.
I suppose it is instinct.
I suppose there is a lot of instinct everywhere,
But that is no excuse.

LOVE

Will they evaporate?
They may.
That is the lovely
End of the white stars:
A blue heaven.
I wish I were a white star
Flying within my red heart,
My red heart within my blue heaven.

All Is Well

: 2019 :

ALL IS WELL

I'm off my noggin, as you see,
And love is truth, and so is she,
The whole of hate is minstrelsy,
A lovely gasp
Of dying.
We fly beyond the sky, you see,
And love beyond capacity,
And turn the corner of the page
As though there were no more to grasp,—
There always is, I reckon.
Future time is past as well,
And all of us are used to Hell,
And wait for nought
To ring the knell
That brings us in or out to tell
What truth can offer to us all,
Love and safety,—
All is well.

JESUS!

You always come back.
You always come back again,
And again and again and again.
And then you die,
And then you come back again.

WE SING

We sing:
Boiling.

We say nothing, only —

Only we wait for love,
Perfection of love, —

It's an ephemeral kiss, isn't it?

THE SAFE SONG

Were the whistle to blow,
It would blow me right out of you,
As though I were being born twice,
Not once, for every eye to see.
And then I would blow you so tight,
So terribly tight like truth,
You'd die not once but twice,
And feel the air like ice,
Blowing right out of me.

SIGHING LIGHTLY IN THE DARK

Save a kiss for the light April air,
And save one for me.
Hold me up by my light yellow hair,
That I may see.

I do not sit on pins
Or drive myself over bumps
In the road as though angry or mad.
No: I am tired but satisfied.

You are my signature, love,
And I follow you
At the pace you set
Walking over the wet terrain
To the end of our long yellow road.

THEY CALLED HER FLOWER

("...non ignara mali,
*   miseris succurere disco...")*

Asters and Zinnias,
Blue forget-me-nots,
Sweet Alyssum,
Calendula and pink Columbine,
These combine to plant the garden
Of my mind,
As though their scent
Would never lose
Its touch.
Fall! Don't leave
Me grieving on the vine,
All flowers pass,
And so do I,
And so do I.

IF ONLY FOR A DRINK

Will you drink
A tun of tea
And see apostrophes?
Our future's drowned
In love foresworn
With elemental ease.

DITTY

Tears fly,
Flies rend,
Love wastes,
Heads bend.
Teeth grin,
Tongues ply,
I love,
I die.

ARRIVAL/DEPARTURE

Why was it so easy—
Pulling you down
In the yellow light
Like pink silk at night,
As soft as skin?
Where was I lying
As I smiled goodbye,
As I looked above,
And the sky darkened?

I make myself alone,
And cry tears down.

TEARS HOT, TEARS COLD

Lavender tears
Greet love or loss,
Hot love tears
Made sweet by bees,
Collecting warmth
From tulip trees,
Or falling down like frozen leaves
Or icicles from icy eaves.

LIP SHIFT

Will you miss me in the morrow?
I am sad
And you are sorrow.
Sing a tune—
"I will tomorrow"—
Cannot now
For lack of one thing,
Black the love
That loves alone.

HIDING IN THE LIGHT

I am the shadow of what there is,
And the suitor in waiting of what can't be.

BLACK AT DAWN

Love learns to fault itself
In time its embassy foreclosed;
There is no way to wager back:
Death hides behind the rose.

TAKE HELP FROM BOTH SIDES

I make my brain
   work slowly by the by.

I carry myself straight
   beneath my chin.

I write beneath the weight of words—
   As though they could make anything—

I know they could, like little mice,
   Never pausing to look twice

Across the road, before they cross
   Beyond the snow, beyond the ice,

That makes me think
   They should look twice.

PRELUDE AND PERFORMANCE

Kiss me, prelude.
Fly by night
And see what you see.

I am larger than you
When it counts,
And can find myself
In the smallest opportunity.

LOVE BY INCREMENTS

Strike in the sun, lad!
Don't take love so seriously.
The body will respond,
And if the girl is prompt to be had,
—TAKE HER!

CURBSIDE

Twenty-five? You want
Twenty-five?
What a limit!
When the heart speaks
Volumes,
VOLUMES!

LIVING EXTENSIVELY

I can't hear,
I can't hear,
Alone in Space
And in the Air.

You can hear me
From below,
Truth beguiles us
As we float
Outside the limits
Of our eyes—
Now we'll live
Where love survives
Beyond the bounds
Of wild surmise.

INFINITY

A touch of green
Gives a row
Of wavy palms
Time to grow
As fast as weeds:

To catch a breeze
With heads above
And touch with ease
Infinity,
The source of all and none
In one:
Of what there is—
Or never was.

RICH TEXT

I have broken
All the boundaries—
Will you follow
Me?

THE SKIN OF EEL

Hopefully slightly longer,
Pull my toe and see,
Add seasoning that is stronger
Than an oyster at sea with me.
The salt is for our toast,
And pepper serves to roast
A rooster on its roost,
Preparing not to feel
The shiny skin of eel
That wraps its tongue around
The ectoplasmic sound
Of feet upon the ground.

HONEY-SUCKLE

There is more than one way
To arrive at night:
Turn the faucet on,
And it will pour out jellibies,
Pink posies and other delights.
Seat yourself under the running water,
And you will catch the scent
Of honey-suckle the hue
Of delicate yellow amber,
Cups of white and gold nectar,
Sweet drops like sugared teas,
Iris eyes and loosestrife,
And whorls of primrose
Pink and white—
Come taste two drops with me!

YOU RUN SLOWLY DOWN

A desert of one:

Turn by here,
And if you are
One of the tropical kind,
You will be running like a mimosa
Into the sand.

RESURRECTION

We are back-to-back
And don't know it.

Where is the pleurisy now?

I am thinking
We are all clean:

And so we are
—All of us.

DISAVOWING THE LAST

Blue at last!
I say, Blue at Last!

Stretching out to the horizon of grace,
Pouring flowers out of guns disarmed by roses.

I am not going to sleep tonight.

Heliogabalus is wearing blue like the nightshade.

FREEING THE OYSTERS

It's my cook.
He takes off his shoes,
Rubs his toes with laughter
And prepares all his dishes
For disaster.
"We abhor blood,"
He says,
Plants his toes
In the soup-pot
And produces a big red ooze,
Then loosens his collar,
Calms his followers,
And wanders within the possibility
Of perpetual dynasties of oysters
Protected by mother-of-pearl
From strikes by gulls.

Sand, anyone?

OFF WE GO

Perhaps you have been caught
In the truth for a change.
The alarm rings,
The eyes weep for wisdom,
And the gray heavens close
Overhead as if the people below
Will never again see their shadow,
The pain it brings,
Or the pall love brings
To their last leave-taking.

NIGHT SONG

You remain lost
Under the moon:
That traitor sings
For his evening's delight
Between dusk and dawn—
The sun will soon rise
To extinguish his song.

TOUR OF THE FORTUNATE

Put your hand there, darling,
That feels so good.

We should meet
More often in the hood.

Pleasure is the means
We measure

Love—
And heat the means we keep

To measure us.

TO A WILD ROSE

While you sweat, dear,
Sweat tears raw,
You will find that love is mine, dear,
Love is mine and dross apart.
Heave the apple in my heart, dear,
Out to see the world apart.
Trouble leaving?
Don't you fret! dear,
We are one and love
One too:
I say again—
We are two and one.
So tip your head
Where lies try hate, dear,
Split apart the two who won,
Lies and lies and lies and lies:
You a lawyer!
Bittersweet, dear,
Bitter, Bitter.

Now I turn my head to sleep,
I pray the Lord my soul to keep,
Sister, darling, where you go now?
Who you two dear,

Who am I?

I love you still, dear,

Like the rain here,
Sweet drops of Heaven,
Hair like flax,
I am old now,
Flowing old now,
Left to rot now (Lawyer Lot)

1. Sister love me!
2. Lawyer love me!
3. Brother love me!
4. Defense away!
5. Away! Away!
6. Away! Away!
7. And Now I Dead!!!!!
8. Away! Away!

WHERE HE GO, THAT MAN?

Up the inseam,
In the morning,
Always scorning
Love 'n Love.
Why you listen,
Little Chil'ren,
When our love
Is not enough?
We will offer
Food for offal,
Black gar'bahge
Auf wiedersehen!

ILLUSTRIOUS PLUM

Illustrious,
Industrious
Fruit of the womb's
Declining fire,
We would have your
Random tempo,
Lavender
The merest name.
We will take you
By the hand
And see you safely
Recondite,
We must show
The world you're safe
And so are we,
Man, so we are.

YELLOW UMBRELLA

How you cover
All our trumps
And truthful lies,
Manufacture
Every fracture
In the scope
Of tongue's device.

We will come back
Seriozny*,
Save us from
Ourselves at last,
Barrier of language
Languish,
Truth is uni-
versal too!

*Russian for "serious".

SLEEP'S CANON

White queen, black queen,
Yellow queen, too,
What you all in queendom do?
There is plenty food
For heavy
Lifter
In the trash
That's blue.
We do sifter
Like a Lister
Wash our mouth
And teeth
Anew. —
Give us time
And temper tasteful
Worship
Tongue—
And Truth, You too!

LED BY THE NOSE

Reliable, he's falling down reliable,
Lawyer for the dirty cow,
Argue fully
all the woolly
facts and features—
We know you!

Take a creature
By the nostrils
Put a ring therein
to speak,
Pain awakens
hollow follow
Where you lead
alack alack.

Third from back
Behind the eight ball
Move atrocious
Motion, too,
See what's empty
Up above, below
Is lost to
Filthy crew.

ALLO!

Put your head on backwards, darling,
Truth turns empty right away.
Smoking green grass, direct envy,
Dreams abscond with wit and will,
Polar bears apportion mercy,
Take the light
And hang it up.
Shadow white
Is like the snow, dear,
Rumpelstiltskin flax a lot,
Toes are nimble,
Toe-nails glitter,
Love's a lasso, Inwigo.

GOOD-BYE!

Turn your body
Like a pretzel,
Eat at both ends
Like a peach,
You will have
No curvature, dear,
Only salt, dear,
Only salt.

A BIG MATISSE

He big, Matisse!
Blue, bright, yellow, red,
Sight unseen,
Tired queen,
Apple strudel,
In the rough,
Apple strudel
That's enough!

PLUNKETT

He will swerve by me,
That Plunkett E,
Label of the frost
And the deadpan WE,
We are no one person
In Love with me,
I ain't it an' you ain't me.

COOL FRACTURE

Fracture the Fairy Tale here, my dear,
We swim up North where the coast is clear,
Are stones rocks
And is life dear?
Sell me down the river
When the coast is clear.

Don't misjudge intent, my wife,
I've loved you once (or maybe twice),
Love can cool (and so can ice),
Touch my tongue with strange device.

The electric shock will take you down
Below the middle like a punching clown,
Don't dent my head, said the pugilist,
Time can be short: and so can this!

"GET DEMOBBED!" SHE SAID.

I am out at last, he said,
Out of the washroom and the basin, too,
There's no cheap step to learn anew,
Birds fall off trees and into you!

Take your bird and bring it back
To life and limb in a gunny sack,
It will dance in thanks to you,
Dance and dance and dance like new.

Poor bird doesn't know where it will go,
The gunny sack hides a gun or two,
Hands in two for me and you,
We'll shoot our bird and make it stew.

Eat and eat and eat our stew,
We eat flesh and fowl and few
Appear to love us as we do,
We'll starve tomorrow, as for now:
You'll do.

ONE WHOLE CHRONICLER OF THE RACE

What you have by hand, she say?
Purpose lost and purpose fraught.
Love has come and sure she may—
Sure she lose and sure she's caught.

Blue and green and white and red.
What was that the parrot said?
I am you and you are who?
Me! I say and fall in two.

Two are more than two sometimes.
What a gas and what two crimes?
We are cronies of a sort.
Take a snort and fly good-bye.

O! my dear, what do you do?
How can I and how can you!
We are only one by one,
Set aside that aspergum.

Now we turn to see the sun,
It's hiding, too, it sees so clear,
Every day of every year,
It always sees, poor blinking seer.

A lovely time was had by all.
Up till a rain storm cast a pall
Upon the sun that was such fun,
Now we're gone and fun's undone.

ECTOPLASMIC

Ectoplasmic:
I looked the meaning up—
And it fell down.

Apples will pick you up.
Apples are full of 1) wisdom
Or 2) guile.

We park our minds at night.
Sometimes at night we sleep.
Sometimes day talks to us
In the night
And keeps sleep away.

What is awry?

Away.

HOME

I feel I am waking for the first time.
I feel I am waking myself up.
It is odd, sleeping.
It doesn't know who it is.

It erases itself as soon as it
Begins to find out.

You, my baby?
Who are you?
Where do you sleep
But in my mind?
When I wake up,
You vanish
Like salt in the sea
That looks for a place to sit
At the very bottom of things.

Sometimes we want to go home,
But where is that?

SONG 1

The morning rings a tune aloft,
Hey diddle diddly
My son John

Turns his face to face the throng
Hey diddle diddly
Now he's gone;

Love him miss him art all gone
Where can we find
What we have lost?

Hey diddle diddly
Lost alone,

Now we pitch our tent above,
And find new friends
To sing with us,

Hey diddle diddly
Sing with us!

BREATH OF FEAR

Try us on for size, my dear,
The water's warm
And so are we

The level-headed ne'er come near
Afraid of truth
And minstrelsy.

Fool here, fool here,
What do you fear?
The breath of Truth
The breath of fear.

Amber is your face come clear
As you die slowly
Breath of fear!

A CURE

Lovers lost
And love to gain
Seems to nourish
Where we are

Where we are
And how we move
But never leave
Behind our love

Patience is the key to love
And love is key
To life aloft

Fly above life
Tempest tossed
And life we love
Though tempest tossed.

Turn me over
On your back
Turn you over
Back alack
Red and white and blue and green
Love is punctured
I can't see

Now I see you
By my side,
Love is heated
So are we
Like a wife or two we see
We are cured
And show me two!

THE BANDIT AND THE PERICOLE

The danger, my dear,
Is in your ear
You cannot hear
A safety net

Of filigree
It holds you up
And so do I
With love to puncture
So do I.

PANJANDRUM

What do you see here
Panjandrum?
Love stays quiet:
Me alone

Open love
And open lost
Upon the lee
Of Ocean tossed

I love me
And all alone
So love falls
And so do you

Turn me over
On my side
I am living last alive
Last alive, so fast alive,
Die away
So last alive.

BLEU

Hand me down
My light to see
Turn my eyes
Upon the tree
Of life, its limb
To fall below
The wind doth blow
Blow wind blow
And fall below!

WHERE O WISDOM?

Where O Wisdom man you lie?
On the shore by my left eye?
Are you blind — as blind as I?
Save me from the love that dies, oh my.
Love is dying in my wake,
I sleep alone and sleep awake,
I am both and you mistake
Sleep alone and sleep awake.

LIFE LOST

Temper tries to burst at last
The temporal bonds of blackened cast
Surrounding pale the willow weeds
The widow wears her grief to ease:

Her care is new, her heart still numb
With love to lose and none to come,
By close shadows she must lie,
In undeserved perfidy.

Turn her body by the by,
What was pretty now must vie
With canker sores and worms inside,
She'll hope that Latter Days arrive.

PRODIGAL

The word is chaste
That I do know,
The crown is false
Upon your brow,
The gold is dross
And breath too low
To carry out
What I do know:
Love can hate itself to hark
Beyond the bounds
Of horny bark.

O love, you left me
In your thrall
And now you find me
Prodigal.

A JOHN

I stream, and consciousness follows
Spell me, and my dog pees on me
Like a cloud floating above the sun.
The clouds of pain are hollow
And love does not follow
In their footsteps,
Even John of Salisbury
Would wonder
About me...

ELEPHANT

No, the kitchen is not the coolest room
In the closet,
The penumbra of thought
And pain of hiding:
We are so tearful
In the night
As the slaughter continues
And my lives mount
To my head.
Who is in the bracken
By the aisle listening,
The path to epiphany
Phantasy of Heaven?
Love, O Love, What have you done to me?
Where were you
When I died all at once?
Now I ride the night
Like a stick
And the Watchman Cometh
And the Iceman speaks to me
In sparkles slow glistening.
Yes, I am not possible any more,
The past is vanished
L'Estrange is Sovereign
No light shows itself
Beneath the crime's black head.
We walk gingerly

Beyond Sun- and Moon- Joy,
Trip o'er your own feet
And fall down dead.

TERRIBLE TRUTHS

Death will take me
Before I die.
I wonder wonder
Who am I?

AMBER MOTES

Trial by fury.
The jury of the mob
Will prove to extinction
That you were once well,
Now you are only a little star
Trying to keep from going out
Of style.

PLOTINUS' EMANATIONS

What I was looking for—
Why I created—
It was myself—
A love
For myself.

CHARACTER STORE

Place your lips on mine, my dear,
To say goodbye to me.
I love to feel your breath on mine,
Test of perjury:
The end of time comes up behind
Where we can't see
To save ourselves—
To go below where nothing moves—
Behind a frozen sea.

DANCE, DEAR

Rasp while you will, my love.
Your tongue grates mine
As we both fall into
The arc of Time
Without seeing out front
Or behind—just plopped down
In space like a fairy or leprechaun
Dancing a fox trot
Fast
Like two spirits
Meant for each other.

NOTHING, MY LOVE

I am ready to kill myself by accident.
I am ready to throw out smoke
In perpetuity.
I am a mouth full of dead snakes
And eucalyptus trees—
Then nowhere,
Because that is where we will end up
Beyond the end of our comfortable Universe:
NOTHING will not find us there,
Because the only true thing
You can say about nothing is that
It does not exist.

So where are you today, dear?

PINSTRIPE

What you hiding there, God?

Pin-stripe?
Lucre? Luxury limited to the atmosphere?
What atmosphere?
Like we find on Venus?
She dead and dry, that fat lady.
She a smoking relic of an empty planet.
No more love, honey.
No more sweets for you.
I am going to melt you down
and eat you for dessert
until you live on nothing but
my smoking gut.

At least earth has four elements.
And Venus?
—Nox est perpetua una dormienda.

At least she's got something up her sleeve.

HELLO, MAN

I am not anxious to die all at once,

But maybe I will.

Kick the sill over,
raze the house,
Pour blood into the cellar,
the root of my behavior
that fills up red and orange,
Then, as I get used to the coming night—
I weep to you and try,
try to say goodbye....

DEAD

Dead, I tell you he's dead.

Lost in the primrose tree.

A man in a fix. Touring through alabaster canyons of the head.

I should have known.

You?

Yes. It's expected of the Almighty.

Is that you, darling?

I'm waiting for you. Up in the tree
Beside me. Come see. The moon is up, and the sun will soon follow.

Well, there she is.

I told you.

You are brilliant.

From time to time, and outside time sometimes. O! I have put my foot in it again. Where the dog goes, there go I. Always. Don't you know? Always. I am sliding around this way as though I could tell the end of everything all at once.

A pilgrimage into knowledge. Now you are beginning to understand me.

It isn't hard.

Not at all.

Limp.

Limping through the graces of Heaven.

Who is going to get us out of this place?

Will will.

It helps.

And the bard?

He's hard, too.

TURTLE DOVE

Now I can carry my life
On my own head

—The Voice of the Turtle

SWEET PRINCE, I CANNOT SEE

Exacerbate the will,
What's well will fill us still,
Torment the Tommy
If you can
By slipping by
At 10pm,
And then you'll have
Another foe
To play with you
Beneath the elm,
Where sheep and chickens
Spend the night
And cocks can crow
When morning comes,
To greet the night
Dear reader,
Be like me,
And turn your head
Where it can see
The purple dawn
And purple heart
Of every soldier
In the dark;
Take us there!
And leave us, too,
Both one of me
And two of you,
We splinter like
A stick or 2

That holds the body
Of the Christ;
He is gone,
And we are too,
And soon the sun
Will follow moon
And leave behind no light at all:
That is how we close our song!

HELLO

That's when I was normal
Long ago. Now I seem to be
Floating in air like a solitary
Island away from you

Into the Blue Sky.

BIRTHDAY

Truth is mirth —
A drunken holiday.
And all the guests agree:
I was meant for you, my dear,
And you abolished—
me.

RUN LIKE A HAWK

And eat the meat you like:
Bears are crisp
And sleek as eels
Nothing sweats like two swift deals
Of brownish trout
Along the trail
We wander on:
We follow in the wake
Of every child
That crosses water
By himself—
And finds the other side—
O, do not say
What do you mean,
I am just a silly queen
That ponders fate
At darkest noon
And soon avoids
The bats that swoon
Once sun has set
Beyond the moon,
And night arrives—
A canker room.

PRINZ OF THE REALM

Silly putty,
Lead me onward,
Turn me out of true,
What was once
Is now forgotten
Masses of
The race.

(What a mess!)

Clean it up man,
Before it eats us,
—a poison dream.

What a mess!

DALI

Sometimes my eyes burn and my ears go on strike.
How rue floats through the air
And enters my head
As though there were nothing already there!
Read yourself inside
And see what's left.
A little froth,
A fat moth or two,
And a nose sitting in a wounded chair.
How do we convalesce after
A war of words?
Saints can live on truth.
The rest of mankind
Must sleep like stones
Released from the roof of the world
Just as though the end were near —
And it is —
Nearer than anyone might think,
Melting like a cake of ice
That we realize too late
Will bring everything to a halt.
Turn yourselves around, O people,
Face the facts:
Nothing will be left but trash
When you have closed up shop.

READYMADE

The moon shines outside the door.
I am hard at work
But I love the moon
Enough to live in its shade.

APOLOGIA

Aeons ago I fell from grace,
And now I am returning to my anointed place.

THE END OF TIME

This is where
All my time must go,
To Paradise alone,
Running about Death's throne:
Dark, cold stone.

PINCKNEY BORN AGAIN

There is only one:
A tall white corpse
Hanging in the air,
Vibrating in my memory.
My feet stand
On the outer rim of the world,
as though there were
no other place to be.
I thought I was tired,
but I'm only a little wasted,
a little frayed,
a big man like me,
wasted and traveling
toward death,
another world,
just the end,
and a fragrant new beginning.

WASTE

Lollipops spring into my head
As promiscuously as daisies,—
Or dandelions with claws.
You slow me down
With an unborn life,
Offering only promises
Empty of love,
Standing on nothing
Like an albatross.

REVELATION

The suns
Are coming out of hiding.
They talk to each other in whispers,
In more than one heaven,
As though their Universe were multiple.

It's Christmas,
And I am sending myself to the moon,

Who sometimes stays out
Later than he should.

He is cold, the moon,
And could use a little more
Skipping around.

HOLY LOVE

So you don't approve of me?
You don't approve of my poetry.

Who are you?

You take up space beside me.

You are without eyes,
And I continue
To live in Paradise.

I am touching you somewhere.

I think I can see you now!

What force!
What power!

But I am not afraid…

Our Love is not afraid,
Though sometimes,
Intervening between us,
It scares the b'Jesus out of me.

PAINTING THE LADY IN A BLUE TRELLIS

She would have put you down
For a pint
If you could drink it:
Blood as red as the rose,
And green as you,
Staring into the face of a bloom blue true.

What will Nature make of you, of me?
A memorial of painted leaves,
Painted for us, delicately?
We serve as our own natures' canvas
Above ground,
And, reduced to ash,
Make room
For new loves to grow.

Put your lips
Where your eyes touch mine,
Brow upon brow.

Slowly I make you feel me hard.
Then we see where all touching leads,
New red, new green, new blue,
New love straight up,
Up to the sky,
New love,
Blue true.

LOVE HAS ITS COLORS, TOO

Let my spectacles love whom they wish,
upside down on me.
Love can hide behind itself,
by reason if need be,
Inviting possibility
for those who can't love me.

LOSING

I turn to you
In misery and try to mock
You more; we admire
The moon's cool rays
And make the sun's rays warm.
There is no path to follow now
Where once we used to roam.
There is no love to show me still
Where I once had a home.

JEWEL OF A CARRIAGE

Will you put me in a glass
For every eye to see?
Love is hateful,
Hate lies faithless,
Sitting in the sea.
Feet can wander,
Torn asunder,
Left or right, I don't care.
All a chaos,
Lost in darkness,
Buckled at the knee.
Toes are tempting
Ways for stalking—
Show them where to roam.
My love's endless
Like the precious
Jewels we carry home.

TO ALICE

So, Alice, where are you standing
Now? Where do you wear your brow?
Understanding more love than mine,
Sweet love like me,
Alice, trying hard
Not to move a stone,
Not to be the stone
That moves alone
Outside my ken
And throne
Of Jasper stone:
The end we always see
Of what we know can't be
Forever and alone—
So close
And so alone.

THE LOVER ESCAPES

The love is chaste
That I now know,
The crown is false
Upon my brow,
The gold is dross
And breath too low
To carry out
What we do know:

Love can hate itself and bend
Beyond the bounds
Of its own end.

O Love, I left you
In my thrall,
And now I find you
Prodigal.

PREMATURE

Time to lie, my lolling head,
Time to sleep, time for bed,
You'll keep me company, sweet head,
And lie with me upon the bed
Of night,
As though there were
No more to say.
I know there isn't in the wave,
I'm not afraid of you, kind knave,
I've lived with you and now will die —
I'm not afraid of where you wait
And I will lie,
Unafraid of where we'll die.

THE HEAD

My artist slides,
With speckles, too,
A spot along
A million too.

Inspection
Of my head I see
And wonder
What is new with me:

There's nothing new
That I can see,
I watch you, too,
As you watch me.

THE ARTIST: FEMME ASSISE

She saw you by the lap,
And tapped you by the head,
And listened to the cockle bird
Fleeing on ahead

We'll all be gone by sunset
With no Savior on the way:
Freedom gives us passage
Through the pains of every day.

FORGIVE THE RIGHT AND LEFT

Forgive the dolt?
A wavy fool.
He sits upon
An empty stool.

But I know
He gives me pain —
A palsy in my chest again.
His mouth flies up
Beyond his brow
If he sees the sea at all,
I wish he'd look and watch me drown
Upon his knee as he looks down.
— A tiresome fool, without a crown
Or other sign of great renown.
He's just a fool or dolt, I say,
And will not let me have a way
To tire him out
And make him sleep
Upon the shores
Of vasty deep, —
Rather, now, he sleeps alone
Until the sun is on its throne
Again to dry us all —
We'll eat our toes so delicate,
And pamper roses roseate:

Goodbye! sweet dolt, and fairy fool,
You are the message and the tool
To get us all from here to there,
I'll go with you —
But do I dare?
Or: do I dare?

A SWIFT PURCHASE

Own me up
Upon the soil,
Baby mine
O baby mine,
I first rest
But then I toil,
Taking you
To toil with me.

Where is heart beneath my eye,
Dry as cinder in the sky?
Heart is dry beneath my sky,
Try me
Try me
One more time:
I am wretched
by the by.

HELLO, MIRO

Relax, dear,
It's just the axe, dear,
To slice you free, dear,
Of some skin.

Willow wails, seer,
Make it quick, there,
Cannot see, where,
Lordy Lord!

PICASSO BENDS

Silly putty in the rue,
Expansion of the soul,
I'll eat you, dear,
Above the neck
A hairy curvy roll.

HIRING MAN

I want to love
Before I die,
If only Love
Would keep the sky
As blue as you
As you ride by
The edge of eye:
The edge of sky.

HANGING MAN

Will they spend
Their love with you?
 Hey nonny nonny
 And a shot of gin.
I am you and you my twin.
 Love abroad
 And love within,
I love me and me love sin,
Sex is healthy
 For a healthy skin.
 Hair falls out
Oh dear, my twin?
 I lose my looks
 And beard my chin.
Gray then white
Once black now prim
Fair exchange
For a hanging slim.

I drink milk
Then turn to gin.
I'll drink myself
For a silky skin.

Babies cry
Both out and in —

Stroke stroke stroke!
That's Him.

ARISE, CHAGALL

Promise sweet
And pretty too,
I bring new
And you bring two.

BARLEY CORN

Trust the simple,
Take him out,
Let him lie
As if in doubt
Of who he is
And where he went
And lost the scent
Of barley corn;
He's the Savior,
And remember
How he plays
The role of Saint.
Rejoice! Rejoice!
Rejoice! Rejoice!
He must take
The role you hate.
Thank you, Judge!

HALFWAY THERE

Halfway there and blown to bits.
Eat the breakfast oats and grits.
Milk the cow upon the rill,
Stone the Man and cook to kill.

It is lovely time for love:
Spring unravels later on.

I am empty,
We are spent.
Spend a quarter, then a cent.

What you want, you silly doll?
I'm no whore,
You're not a moll.

Play with ladies,
Play with me,
Underneath the hanging tree.
Come along and turn me loose,
I'll raise your hackles,
Pretty goose.

Lovely goose-down gives us pause,
Come play with me!
Come play with me!
Very wary willow was.

TRASHED

Hello, Daddy,
Are you surviving nicely?
Do you fill the black vacuum
Of my inner rage,
Perfecting the contest
Between age and age?
You leave tracks
I cannot follow,
O my little God.
I act and you direct:
I want to play myself
Before I'm dead.
My life is
Your property
Until one of us dies.
It makes no difference
Whether it's you or I.
Why, Daddy, you don't even love me: why?

SIXDENIER

Within the cloister they whisper
under their breaths to themselves
in gray robes
and hoods of scarlet or gold
and braids on the waist
worn for show;
They declaim in the garden
too far away to be heard,
Their hands rise and fall
silently in the light
after Vespers as night falls

I see Cerberus at their door
three paces behind the last
from the sacristy
looking up at the crucifix
with a sigh
Sign of what?
Let him bear it alone

Now it's time for a crack to the right,
Let the taper shine there,
Then you have your answer:
    Three dice for a dime
    a nickel apiece
Cut them out and cast them
one by one

by the stench of the dead pig's belly
you'll see nothing but blind sailors
pilgrims and whores
all undone
from top
to bottom

twice he spoke
but no tongue
I'll play with his eyes,
the wandering Jew

The merry Widow's on her way back
To the secular wardrobe-room
to pick up a new exterior
incomparably superior to the old
What's she now?

A bundle of nerves
Strings from ear to ear
Yellow damask in the rear
makes a pretty sight of her
well-worn dilatory personnage
lateral green
longitudinal red
decked for a fool
born to dread
the fire in winter
in the summer the fog
hides her behind

its pearl of a guise
and make her a sailor
in the dark on leave.

THE BLITHEDALE ROMANCE

I might be good on him,
But I'm not exactly like him.
I hear whispers down the street,
It is my enemies come to get me,
But they will never arrive.
I am a willow invisible
To the damned; the drowned
Are suspect because they
Are no longer alive.
Where does it go from here?
The suit is over, or at least played,
And the whole head
Is hurting beyond endurance.
I cannot move my fingers.
My prick is dense as marble.
I am seeing double rainbows—
It is after the shower now
And yet I am still unfinished.
I know I am safe,
But that means nothing to me.
I want love, I want fame,
I want everything.
I want to die.

Index of First Lines
(The use of italics denotes a first line that is also the poem's title.)

A

A cute little lyric, 55
A Danube? 56
A desert of one, 561
A gift indeed is, 300
A heart is what you have, 337
A hill, green, blue and yellow, 73
A poem exhibits different colors, 10
A pretty variable in life, 276
A short, harsh cry to say hello, 347
A teaser, a dwindling dish, 41
A tone down the corridor, 492
A touch of green, 557
Abuse my nerves! 513
Aeons ago I fell from grace, 616
Align your self with me, 350
Allowed to grow, 329
An eye's body alive, 510
And eat the meat you like, 612
And the poet, 467
Antiquities live off fat, 20
Are you a vision, 77

Are you my memory? 354
Asters and Zinnias, 544

B
Badinage behind the back, 16
Beauty is the beast we all long for, 520
Blood as full, 44
Blue at last! 309
Blue at last! 563
Blue leaf leave me, 15
Blue will teach you, 518
Born by woodbine, 19
Bruegellande, grotesque and ribald, 345

C
Chrysanthemum, why are you blue? 334
Come, and I should play, 400
Commit to love, 122
Customer expense, 171

D
Dead, I tell you he's dead, 605
Dear Lady, 301
Death has a decided, 325
Death will take me, 597
December, month of ice, 491
Dibble-dabble, 498
Did the white swan, 459
Dido died upon the pyre, 25
Do you like me? 74
Dry ice on a wet lawn, 499

E
Ectoplasmic, 582
Elaborate gains, 297
Entirely too blue, you see, she said, 514
Exacerbate the will, 608
Experience importunes my heart, 104

F
Fight for love? 490
First, he will send me his eyes, 488

Forgive the dolt? 631
Forty was my goal, 348
4:30 is the time to die, 258
Fracture the Fairy Tale here, my dear, 579

G
Give him a death's head, 50
Go on, sit down and write it, 128

H
Halfway there and blown to bits, 640
Hand me down, 590
Handy-dandy the milkman, 416
Have you ended our affair? 38
Have you got me now? 455
He big, Matisse! 577
He will swerve by me, 578
Hello, Daddy, 641
Hello, woe, 302
Here in the market, 11
Here we go, behind the blithe pragmatism, 140
Hopefully slightly longer, 559
How you cover, 572

I
I am a map full of particles, 353
I am crying over my incompetence, 147
I am delicious, 251
I am licking licorice, 435
I am never going to be washed again, 67
I am not anxious to die all at once, 604
I am not blind to you, love, 93
I am not supposed to be writing poetry, 533
I am out at last, he said, 580
I am popping about, 143
I am ready to kill myself by accident, 602
I am sad tonight, 404
I am the shadow of what there is, 550
I am thinking, 295
I am waiting, 500
I am waiting for my shadow, 166

I am waiting, patient, 4
I am wandering through the corridors, 215
I am writing like fire, 221
I bought a lot of food, 395
I can write a poem, 469
I can write anything at any time of day, 356
I can't hear, 556
I can't help it, 363
I can't stop, 211
I cannot write, 83
I cry inside, 250
I do not know, 227
I don't feel so driven, 289
I don't know, 155
I don't think, 260
I feel I am waking for the first time, 583
I feel like writing another one, 328
I frighten myself, 149
I have a lion's eyes, 47
I have all the time there is, 237
I have been looking, 213
I have broken, 558
I have to paint, 402
I like the way you move your body, 333
I love you, 249
I love you occasionally, when you answer, 99
I make my brain, 552
I might be good on him, 645
I might lose it, 321
I must understand before I fail, 307
I pitch my ear, 229
I send my soul out, 494
I shall end my days, 63
I should have painted you a long time ago, 169
I stream, and consciousness follows, 594
I think you're right, 168
I tie my ear to a balloon, 7
I try to see, 346
I turn to you, 624
I want time, 64
I want to love, 636

I want to write another poem, 432
I wear life like a cup of tea, 377
I will become ballistic, 262
I will keep writing it, 286
I will live a mandarin, 327
I will not sweat tears for you, 267
I will put you on the little side of laughing, 132
I will turn you in, 167
I will write one more, 497
I would like to feel completely well, 5
I write by looking away, 530
I write poems like water, 53
I'd never seen them there before, 427
I'd rather turn upside down, 193
I'll get it if I need it, 461
I'll never forget the four flights up, 507
I'll start verso obligato, 523
I'll wash them, 114
I'm a dish, 71
I'm off my noggin, as you see, 539
I'm sure, 255
I've got to wear the brown ones, 441
If I keep writing, 440
If I start in on you, 318
If the world were not round, 365
If you can come, 108
If you saved the world, 339
If you want to cash me in, 153
Illustrious, 571
In Brooklyn there are no owls, 326
In Hawaii, 463
In the corner of my room, 503
In the spring, 14
In this perfect world, 481
Is there something wrong with love? 299
It is one o'clock and I am tired, 118
It is probably the time, 522
It is so strange, Creation, 387
It is there, 59
It is time, 344
It is two o'clock, 225

It turns your life upside down, 343
It used to be so easy, 253
It was difficult, 331
It's a gift, 443
It's as though you had fallen into a dream, 80
It's getting late, 183
It's getting warm, 406
It's hot water, 199
It's my cook, 564
It's not my favorite one, 100
It's not supposed to happen like this, 185
It's not too early, 223
It's the red rose, 68
It's the truth, 61
It's too late, 391
It's your brain that cannot see its nose, 408

K
Kill my dog, 161
Kirilenko: fire the innocent, 135
Kiss me, prelude, 553

L
Lavender tears, 548
Let my spectacles love whom they wish, 623
Let us demonstrate how I do it, 351
Let's see, 340
Life is what I do to myself, 471
Lily on my hat, 284
logically marine, 49
Lollipops spring into my head, 619
Look, Mother, 383
Look toward the moon, 124
Love at first sight is irretrievable, 89
Love is a sign, 304
Love is like an instrument, 370
Love learns to fault itself, 551
Love lies a little, 465
Lovers lost, 586
Loving you is a rapture, 412

M

Make me a copy of myself, 285
Mama, I'm firing you, 95
Maybe I can squeeze, 310
Maybe I can work in the morning, 366
Maybe no poem will, 447
Maybe you did give it to me, 62
Most would not deny, 78
My artist slides, 629
My cat understudies, 517
My day is poison, 133
My days continue to decline, 82
My head is open, 280
My life is my gift to you, 76
My soul moves, 428
My survival is without bounds, 157

N

New houses for old, 98
No, the kitchen is not the coolest room, 595
Nothing comes to mind, 263
Now I can carry my life, 607
Now Reason's drowned, 52

O

OK. We'll watch the watch carefully, 145
One afternoon the future, 257
Only fools love themselves, 113
Operator, call 911, 316
Opuscular thoughts through, 516
Orange juice slides down my bib, 189
Orpheus, lute on a string, 24
Our Nemesis is, 532
Out by the gas-house, 17
Own me up, 633

P

Pandora might have known, 69
Papa, you are what I seem, 322
Parlay your tongue, 524
Pearls lie deep, 501

Perhaps you have been caught, 565
Philosophy, 453
Place your lips on mine, my dear, 600
Play against the box, 420
Pleasant lip-sync please, 201
Pleasant, the wind, 410
Please don't tell me, 179
Please turn your ear, 288
Plow upon the stair, 209
Ply me with extinction, 303
Poems fill in the breach, 397
Pray, then Purge, 28
Precipitation tickles, 45
Pretty lupine, 57
Promise sweet, 638
Publish perceptible, 23
Pull up your pants! 268
Pure as pain, dry as ice, 75
Put your hand there, darling, 567
Put your head on backwards, darling, 575

R
Rasp while you will, my love, 601
Red or blue, 335
Regina is the fault, 138
Relax, dear, 634
Reliable, he's falling down reliable, 574

S
Said Sweeney to Mrs. Porter, 12
Sappho was happy, 97
Save a kiss for the light April air, 543
Sculpt me, turn me on the wheel, 8
Sex onomotopoeia, 96
She saw you by the lap, 630
She will just have to wait for her dinner, 120
She would have put you down, 622
Shed your principles, 380
Silly putty, 613
Silly putty in the rue, 635
Slide along the blade, 482

Slight and sly, 489
So, Alice, where are you standing, 626
So: the right wing, 66
So you don't approve of me? 621
Some day I will stop, 373
Some people want the bomb, 493
Someone has come back, 431
Someone I know is, 521
Sometimes I feel a force in me, 324
Sometimes my eyes burn and my ears go on strike, 614
Soon we will go to Zanzibar, 3
Strike in the sun, lad! 554
Suicide is like a life-jacket, 187
Suppose, to start with, 6

T

Tears fly, 546
Temper tries to burst at last, 592
That is General Breed, 42
That's a very nice jacket, 445
That's when I was normal, 610
The arabesque of violence, 283
The artist slides, 528
The baby sleeps at the garage, 217
The bats will be back, 72
The blue in my mind, 414
The brain plays fitfully, 159
The burial of the fly, 231
The cereal is turning brown, 203
The chair crashes into the wood, 109
The coleanthus bears reckoning, 269
The cross-piece of his bow, 51
The danger, my dear, 588
The dime will buy you nothing, 529
The feedback is back, 130
The heat lies low, 278
The laugh is in the swing, 422
The lively amputee, 162
The love is chaste, 627
The moon shines outside the door, 615
The moons are perilous, 91

The morning rings a tune aloft, 584
The musical air turns wisdom to wit, 9
The new Renaissance man, 21
The night becomes my soul, 26
The night has become empty, 191
The peach tree, 434
The President of the Universe, 252
The round nose, 116
The simplest script, 126
The small family, 438
The soldier moss stands, 483
The street senses the pedestrian, 40
The suns, 620
The word is chaste, 593
The words won't go in, 18
The wounds of time I could not save, 338
Theory. An eye into the dark, 46
There are four nights a week, 195
There are three tribulations to discover, 381
There is a little hint of it, 457
There is a step awry, 367
There is a wild man in my mind, 342
There is more than one way, 305
There is more than one way, 560
There is no way to get around me, 151
There is only one, 618
There is really only one evening star, 336
There is someone staring at me, 48
There is still time to come, 430
There we go, into the night, 102
They are all done, 385
They buffet the wind, 429
They don't know, 451
They have to accept me as I am, 352
This can go there, and that, too, 519
This is a biography, 197
This is my fine paper, 173
This is the sort of fall, 79
This is what I do, 389
This is where, 617
This little man, 320

This play is a rock, 39
This sky is my turn, 60
Three eyes will conquer much, 296
Thrice three makes nine, 54
Through silence, 375
Time: a multiple blow, 330
Time to dine? Nonsense, 509
Time to lie, my lolling head, 628
To save myself, 274
Tracks of ants around the primrose, 37
Trial by fury, 598
Trust the simple, 639
Truth is mirth, 611
Try night on for size, 106
Try tea, 355
Try us on for size, my dear, 585
Trying to hide? 502
Turn Antigone out, 27
Turn your body, 576
Twenty-five? You want, 555

U
Up the inseam, 570

W
Wailing. The blue mountain accompanies, 111
Wait, Mistah! 265
We are back-to-back, 562
We cannot remember, 371
We have to wait until ten o'clock, 361
We sing, 541
We will turn the tale over, 272
We'll all be gone by suppertime, 349
We'll be there soon, 164
We'll see what we want to see, 207
We'll work on it again, 271
Wellspring of the mind, dilute me, 136
Were the whistle to blow, 542
Were they all right, the shadows? 378
Were you my brother, 205
Were you to catch me alive, 264

What are we going to write, 291
What do we see in Apple? 504
What do you see here, 589
What I was looking for, 599
What is the matter, 449
What the fool saw in truth, 480
What was done, 70
What you have by hand, she say? 581
What you hiding there, God? 603
What's inside the head? 393
What's the name of the subterranean, 418
When, first, Liz died, 364
When I arrived at twenty-two, 323
When it rains, 315
When people try to give me tests, 487
Where does all that strength go, 306
Where O Wisdom man you lie? 591
Where there is love, 13
Where will they put me, 472
Wherefore worry? 511
Wherever soil or stone can nourish, 43
While you sweat, dear, 568
White queen, black queen, 573
Who died in April? 357
Who is bailing out of the drink? 141
Who was supposed to come? 58
Who's the dam? 94
Whose are the gags? 219
Why was it so easy, 547
Will they evaporate? 534
Will they spend, 637
Will you accept the blank difference, 527
Will you drink, 545
Will you miss me in the morrow? 549
Will you put me in a glass, 625
Will you sink with me, 308
Will you tell, 525
Within the cloister they whisper, 642
Wonder, put it in your hat, 341
Write each scene, 437
Writing is another country, 531

Y

You always come back, 540
You are dead, 293
You ask me, 508
You can choose the day, 398
You don't want to, 294
You remain lost, 566
You were there, 65
You will use my madness, 506
You, poem, are hanging me, 247
You're building on the ruins, 298
You're going to have to help me, 181
You've got things ordered at the last, 368
Your eyes are marble eyes, 526

Index of Titles

A

A Big Matisse, 577
A Blue Belly for Odysseus, 62
A Blue Time, 412
A Certain Heaviness on the Tongue, 82
A Cold Complaint, 126
A Cure, 586
A Danube? 56
A Declining Star, 336
A Drama of the Plathian Interior, 59
A Dream, 100
A Drink, 257
A Gain on Rain, 45
A Grave Situation, 455
A Greek God, 51
A Green Bird and an Answer, 13
A Hard Rap, 525
A John, 594
A Lie About You, 61
A Little Clip, 320
A Long Key, 10
A Long Walk, 278

A Man Without a Tongue, 321
A Meditation, 402
A Million Spots, 528
A Mystery Slow To Be Realized, 443
A Philosophical Greek, 49
A Plaint, 268
A Plangent Tear, 508
A Pluralistic Universe, 40
A Pragmatic Ideal, 132
A Rough Pass, 422
A Sallow Season, 366
A Shady Terminus, 347
A Short Present, 94
A Short Translation, 519
A Single Summer, 465
A Sip at the End, 420
A Small Box, 69
A Song Aside, 231
A Swift Purchase, 633
A Vision, 159
A Zen State, 530
Aces, 91
Address to a Failed Apocalypse, 93
Advent, 437
Against the Academic, 53
Alabama in Painting, 514
All Is Well, 539
Allo! 575
Amber Motes, 598
Amplification, 197
And for Dessert…, 493
Another End, 249
Antigone, 27
Apologia, 616
Apostrophe, 380
Apple Trip, 504
Are There Strawberries in Heaven? 253
Arise, Chagall, 638
Arrival/Departure, 547
At the Age of Five, 342

B

Babies, 141
Barley Corn, 639
Big Birth, 377
Birthday, 611
Black at Dawn, 551
Blasting, 140
Blessing, 445
Bleu, 590
Blue Leaf, 15
Blue Rotation, 111
Bounce, 145
Breath of Fear, 585
Bruegellande, 345
Buckets of Love, 67
Buying Nothing, 529

C

Chanticleer, 346
Character Store, 600
Christmas, 41
Chrysanthemum, 334
Cold Stone, 72
Collegium Vitae, 113
Color Role, 518
Complaint, 193
Coney Island, 229
Conspire With My Heart, 404
Cool Fracture, 579
Cracking Up, 44
Curbside, 555

D

Dali, 614
Dalliance, 171
Dalliance by the Daisies, 37
Dance, Dear, 601
Dead, 605
Debts, 339
December, 491
Dibble-Dabble, 498

Dido, 25
Disavowing the Last, 563
Disavowing the Mean, 309
Ditty, 546
Doubles, 143
Doubt, 520
Duplicate, 65

E

Ectoplasmic, 582
Elephant, 595
Empty Beside, 286
Empty Hazard, 168
Enemy, 354
Epithalamium, 357
Etwas, Zum Beispiel, 368
Exit at Birth, 398

F

Faces, 375
Family Collage, 58
Fee Simple, 23
Feline Maintenance, 517
Fin de Parti, 306
Floating on the Water, 459
Follow Me, 303
Forgive the Right and Left, 631
Forty, 348
Free for Fame or Fame for Free, 371
Freeing the Oysters, 564

G

General Breed, 42
"Get Demobbed!" She Said, 580
Global Warming, 406
God Can Take Care of Himself, 78
Going Up, 185
Good-Bye! 576
Goodbye, Dog, 166
Gossip Mongers, 16
Grass, 482

H

Ha-Ha's, 74
Halfway There, 640
Halloween, 416
Hanging Man, 637
Hanging on the Ruins of My Nose, 298
Harvest, 483
Hello, 610
Hello, Man, 604
Hello, Miro, 634
Heracleitus Under Water, 20
Here in the Market, 11
Hiding in the Light, 550
Hiding Light, 157
High Tea, 296
Hippocrates, 497
Hiring Man, 636
Holy Love, 621
Home, 583
Honey-Suckle, 305
Honey-Suckle, 560
Hot, 299
Hours of an Age, 385
How We End Up, 151

I

I Am Going, 199
I Am Thinking, 295
I Cry Inside, 250
I Have Saved a Life, 187
I Loll on Lily-Pads, 209
I Must Understand, 307
I Need the Rest, 118
I Rightly Fly, 389
I tie my ear to a balloon, 7
I would like to feel completely well, 5
If I Start in on You, 318
If It Did, I Was Cold, 63
If Only for a Drink, 545
Illustrious Plum, 571

In Hawaii, 463
In Line, 217
In the Chambers of the Dark, 293
In the spring, 14
Infinity, 557
Intemperate Weather, 461
Iraq Compos Mentis, 472
It Doesn't Pay to Go to Princeton Anymore, 95

J

Jesus! 540
Jewel of a Carriage, 625
Johannesburg, 237

K

Kill Me Now, 487
Kiss, Kiss, 490
Kissing a Kiss, 300

L

L'avenir, 356
Laurels, 191
Le Roi des Fauves, 28
Led by the Nose, 574
Left in the Order of Things, 301
Leider, 532
Life Lost, 592
Light Me Up, 225
Lip Shift, 549
Lip-Sync, 201
Lipitor, 294
Liquefaction of the Mass, 260
Listening, 364
Living Extensively, 556
Look, Mother, 383
Looking Back, 302
Looking Up an Old Friend, 205
Losing, 624
Lovage, 71
Love, 534
Love 2, 89

Love by Increments, 554
Love Has Its Colors, Too, 623
Love Is Like…, 370
Lucretia Locuples, 531
Lupine, 57

M

Maidenhair, 98
Malaise, 227
Mandarin, 327
Maybe I Can Squeeze, 310
Mister Apollo, 428
Mother's Day, 2000, 114
My Nocturnal Migrations, 526
My Practical Pentagon, 285

N

Naked, 522
Naked for a Day, 509
Name-Dropping, 55
Night Light, 169
Night Song, 566
Nightcap, 106
No Time Left, 337
No Title for Me, 221
Nonnulla, 325
Nothing, My Love, 602
Now Reason's Drowned…, 52

O

Obligato, 523
Ocean Agonistes, 96
Ode, 133
Ode to Time, 330
Ode to Water, 511
Off We Go, 441
Off We Go, 565
On the Road, 331
One Whole Chronicler of the Race, 581
Operator, 316
Opuscular Thoughts, 516

Orpheus, 24
Other, 506
Our Backyard, 271
Our Rose Poem, 68

P

Painting a Lady, 440
Painting Late, 391
Painting the Lady in a Blue Trellis, 622
Pale Apothecaries, 76
Panjandrum, 589
Papa, 322
Paradise, 297
Passing, 265
Patient Days, 324
Pearls, 501
Peonies, 378
Pepsico Pipelines, Coca-Cola Conduits, 343
Periandros, 162
Period of Treasure, 350
Phasellus Ille Quem Videtis Hospites Ait Fuisse Navium Celerrimus, 83
Philosophy, 453
Picasso Bends, 635
Pinckney Born Again, 618
Pinstripe, 603
Pleasant, the Wind, 410
Plotinus' Emanations, 599
Plunkett, 578
Poetry, 328
Polarization, 291
Politics or the Great Bird, 66
Pope, 50
Possible Tête-a-Tête, 99
Preface to a Play, 39
Prelude and Performance, 553
Premature, 628
Pretty Pike, 164
Primus Inter Pares, 507
Prinz of the Realm, 613
Proceed, Wish, 341

Prodigal, 593
Prolegomena to Any Future Metaphysic, 149
Prolixin, 524
Prunella, 329
Psychopharmaceutical, 252
Pure as Pain, 75

R
Rain as Art, 315
Readymade, 615
Recovering, 211
Regina is the Fault, 138
Rembrandt or Vermeer, 418
Resurrection, 562
Revelation, 620
Revenge, 533
Rich Text, 558
Rose Blind, 64
Rounding Out, 365
Row, 340
Run Like a Hawk, 612

S
Sappho, 97
Saved Beneath the Season, 124
Say Nothing, 263
Sculpt Me, 8
Self Delivery, 513
Self-Portrait, 19
Sex Pain, 333
Shadows of the Evening, 80
Sighing Lightly in the Dark, 543
Signature, 304
Sixdenier, 642
Sleep's Canon, 573
Slide by Me, 47
Snow, 457
Socrates' Apology, 432
Some Day I Will Stop, 373
Song 1, 584
Southampton, 161

Sparrow Fleeing, 395
Specific Gravity, 247
Spring in May, 215
Summer Sunflowers, 429
Summertime, 499
Sweet Prince, I Cannot See, 608

T

Take Help From Both Sides, 552
Tears Hot, Tears Cold, 548
Terminal, 108
Terrible Truths, 597
The Able Man, 223
The Archbishop in Spite of Himself, 492
The Artist: Femme Assise, 630
The Ballistic Partisan, 262
The Bandit and the Pericole, 588
The Bee Dying, 367
The Blithedale Romance, 645
The Blue Parrot, 203
The Book, 467
The Charming Face of Dawn, 189
The Choir of the Mind, 408
The Critic, 393
The Dead Dog, 387
The Dove and I, 435
The Drowned Turk, 400
The Ear-Ring, 120
The End of Time, 617
The Gift, 471
The Head, 629
The Heart's Graces, 122
The Injured Eye, 449
The Kiss, 104
The Lily on My Hat, 284
The Loss, 269
The Lover Escapes, 627
The Lungwort and the Hellebore, 427
The Masked Move, 258
The Mirror and the Mask, 527
The Mourning Doves, 267

The Musical Air, 9
The Name We Never Lose, 494
The New Renaissance Man, 21
The night becomes my soul, 26
The Old Tooth, 251
The Peach Tree Grows, 434
The Phoenix and the Dove, 326
The Pilot, 167
The Pink Period I, 272
The Pink Period II, 274
The Present, 136
The Pyre, 283
The Question, 351
The Rainbow, 276
The Rue Poem, 128
The Safe Song, 542
The Sea-Dragon, 4
The Shadow Poem, 264
The Shy One, 70
The Skin of Eel, 559
The Story of My Life, 179
The Tides, 414
The Title of Discernment, 207
The Trap, 195
The Ultimatum, 363
The Voice of Silence, 381
The Vortices, 335
The Wan Ride, 289
The Wounds of Time, 338
Then the Full Love, 481
There We Go, 102
They, 352
They Called Her Flower, 544
They Don't Know, 451
This Sky Is My Turn…, 60
Thrice Three Makes Nine…, 54
Time Again, 353
Time In, 153
Time Is Falling Down, 135
Time to Beguine, 12
"Tityre, Tu Patulae Recubans Sub Tegmine Fagi…", 79

To a Wild Rose, 568
To Alice, 626
To His Love, 109
To His Muse, 213
Tour of the Fortunate, 567
Tragedy Turns Away, 173
Trashed, 641
Traveling Light, 219
Trees, 43
Trouble, 500
Trouble Spots in the Field of Vision, 48
Troubles Leaving, 288
True Tooth, 6
Try Tea, 355
Trying to Hide? 502
Turtle Dove, 607
Twins, 503
Two by Four, 77

U

Underground, 489
United Untied, 255

V

Vertical Alert, 510
Vision, 46
Visions Out of Africa, 469
Visiting Time, 430

W

Waiting/Repulsed, 155
War, 183
Waste, 619
We Sing, 541
We Walk Down the Strand, 447
Wednesday's Treasures, 130
Well, 323
What Do You Remember? 147
What My Love Will Send to Me, 488
What the Fool Could Tell, 480
What They Didn't Want, 438

What We Wish, 73
What Will Happen? 344
Where Am I? 431
Where Did He Go? 349
Where He Go, That Man? 570
Where O Wisdom? 591
Who There Is, 280
Whose Horseman? 181
Will You Sink With Me? 308
Woe, 116
Words in Winter I, 17
Words in Winter II, 18
Work, 397
Working Out Parallels, 521

Y

Yellow Umbrella, 572
You Run Slowly Down, 561
Your Answer? 38
Youth and Age, 361

Z

Zanzibar, 3

CPSIA information can be obtained
at www.ICGtesting.com
Printed in the USA
LVHW091935220321
682108LV00023B/782/J